Sexual
Confidence

By the Same Authors

———

HOW TO FALL OUT OF LOVE

Sexual Confidence

DR. DEBORA PHILLIPS
WITH
ROBERT JUDD

Houghton Mifflin Company Boston

1980

Library of Congress Cataloging
in Publication Data
Phillips, Debora.
Sexual confidence.
Includes index.
1. Sex.   I. Judd, Robert, joint author.   II. Title
HQ31.P59   306.7   80-14853
ISBN 0-395-29479-7

Printed in the United States of America

P 10 9 8 7 6 5 4 3 2 1

The authors are grateful to Lois Wyse
for permission to quote her poem "The Permissible No."

TO BILL

Acknowledgments

This book has many sources and I am only one.

It was my students (at Princeton University and at Temple University Medical School) and the people at seminars and lectures across the country and those who have come to me for therapy who have helped me to see the need for a new sexual revolution. Their dissatisfaction and disappointments, the depth of their need for intimacy, love, and joyous sexuality, their questions and their problems led me to *Sexual Confidence*. It is a book meant to answer the needs they so courageously made so clear.

In many important ways this is the Reverend Dr. William Kirby's book. His ideas and concepts appear on page after page. I hope I have managed to relay some of his humanity and humor as well. As a colleague, minister, and sex therapist, he has built much of the intellectual foundation for *Sexual Confidence*. His encouragement and support have helped to build the rest.

Bill Phillips is a primary source. Scientist, artist, and editor, he has made contributions of logic and substance that are at the very heart of *Sexual Confidence*. Bill spent endless hours of his valuable time giving the book clarity and strength — qualities he has in abundance.

Professor Nancy Weiss freely lent her historical perspective and her scholarly, painstaking capacity for detail in editing. Her humor and leveling sanity and broad scope are other gifts to be found in these pages.

Dean Carol Thompson, a wise woman with a graceful intellect, swept our concepts clean of wobbliness and pretentiousness. Her brave and rigorous mind opened windows everywhere.

Dr. Joseph Wolpe, pioneer and father of behavior therapy and my teacher, led us so far that all of us follow in his footsteps. His development of desensitization was an essential primary step that made sex therapy possible. His influence, seen in many of the techniques of *Sexual Confidence,* goes far beyond the scope of any single book.

I want to pay a special tribute to David Harris, who was brave enough to risk this book in Boston. And whose gentle humor and powerful intellect is always a source of strength.

To B. J. Foster I owe a special debt of thanks for making difficult tasks seem easy — simplifying my life at the expense of complicating hers.

And, as always, none of this would have been possible without Teresa Holeman and Aurelia Bolling.

DEBORA PHILLIPS
Princeton, New Jersey

Contents

PART THREE SHARING

Sexual
Confidence

1

The New Sexual Revolution

A teen-ager slides his hand under his date's blouse. She tenses, afraid to stop him, afraid to let him go on. A wife leans forward in bed to switch off the eleven-o'clock news. She leans back and waits. Numb with habit, bored by repetition, she and her husband silently "make love." A twenty-eight-year-old woman, feeling uneasy and unhappy, looks across the restaurant table at her date. He has just asked her to go to bed with him, not because he wants to but because he feels it's expected of him. She has just said yes, not because she wants to but because she feels it's expected of her.

Two college students, living together, finish studying for the evening. They take off their clothes; she lies back on the couch. Without kissing or caressing or a word of affection, he puts his penis inside her vagina.

Something is wrong.

Years ago the "pill" promised a sexual revolution. The idea of changing sexual values worried most people. And yet you couldn't help being intrigued by the new freedom the pill was going to bring.

Part of the pill's promise was that you could have sex for its own sake, without emotional entanglements. If you could just brush aside your misgivings a whole new playground was open to you.

But of course you can't just brush aside a lifetime of feelings. Lessons learned in your parents' home or in the schoolyard, however out of date they may seem now, stay with you. The Victorian age ended generations ago. Yet a Victorian hangover of shame and guilt about sex lingers on. In sharp conflict, the idea that more sexual skill and freedom bring more happiness has become a part of our popular culture. Magazines and sex manuals with recipes for pleasure promote this simple theory. Be a better performer, they say, and forget your inhibitions.

Never have there been more sex films, sex magazines, and sex books. Never has there been more casual sex and more sexual variety. And yet, in the midst of all this sex, people are sexually unhappy — longing for intimacy and affection — and finding instead empty, lonely sex.

Sexual freedom and skill are not enough. Sex is simply not that simple.

Counseling and teaching, I talk to thousands of people all across the country about sex. And time after time I see a gap between people's expectations about sex and their own experience.

Let me give you one extreme but poignant example of where the sexual revolution has led us. In a famous metropolitan swingers' club, nude men and women wander across the dance floor and lounge beside the pool, their eyes appraising each other's bodies. They cannot talk except in one- or two-word phrases, because the blare of disco music obliterates conversation. A woman approaches a man, smiles, and leads him to a cubicle, where they will "make love." They both hope for an intense erotic experience. They will both probably be disappointed. For what is missing here and in the "sexual revolution" is romance, courtship, seduction, intimacy, affection, depth, communication, caring, friendship, dignity, and love. What they do have is their technical skill or "performance." But even there, they may have trouble. Deprived of what makes us human, and reduced to genitalia, many men, for example, have difficulty in having erections, their penises limp testimony to what happens when you try to divorce your sexuality from the rest of yourself. For those two people, at least, the sexual revolution has reached a dead end.

Naked strangers trying to "make love" are an extreme example. But they are not very different from couples going to bed on the first date. Or from couples who have forgotten or never learned the pleasures of courtship and necking and going slowly. Or from couples who have never learned how to laugh in bed and say what their fears are and what is good and what is not working.

The sexual revolution hasn't reached as far as it may seem. Men's magazines still soldier on, month after month, with centerfold pictures of casual, opulent sex. Yet sex without intimacy or caring is, by its very nature, a shallow, impoverished experience. On the one hand, there appears to be a broad permissiveness for instant sex and for all kinds of sexual experimentation. On the other hand, there is inevitable guilt and anxiety when people try to do what their feelings tell them not to do. The result of that conflict is lonely, mechanistic sex.

Not that there aren't important changes. There are. Sophisticated contraception means less fear of unwanted pregnancy and less need for abortions. More people are living together outside of marriage, gays enjoy more freedom, there is more bisexuality (especially among women). There really are more options and people are taking advantage of them.

The women's movement has made great changes in the way women see themselves. In many ways women are more assertive. And they are opening up areas that were closed to them. Yet in the bedroom, they are often inhibited and shy and still believe in sexual myths. And now many women, in focusing on orgasms, emphasize performance as much as men do.

And men, while they have been relieved of some of the male burden of always having to take the lead, are often confused. Their old macho role has been discredited. But they still focus on performance — rushing to bed and rushing to intercourse, as if that were the goal of making love. Without a "men's movement" to teach them sensitivity and tenderness, men don't know what's expected of them in lovemaking. The "new woman" threatens them. Often men are the target of a woman's anger when what they really need is empathy. Roles may be changing, there may be more sex — but there is still very little communication between men and women.

What I see now is sex without intimacy, sex without pleasure: people trapped in destructive, repetitive habits, doing things they don't want to do, uncertain and afraid to try the things they'd like to do — men needing to know more about the sexuality of women, women needing to know more about the sexuality of men.

What I propose now is a new sexual revolution: a sexual revolution called sexual confidence, in which sex is a magnificent emotional adventure as well as a delicious physical pleasure. For as complex as is the physiology of sex, the physical pleasure is only the beginning.

We are now just beginning to emerge from the mechanical age of sex. We are now just beginning to realize that measuring and emphasizing performance in sex is just as oppressive as were the old Victorian taboos of shame, secrecy, and silence.

The revolution I propose is a gradual one. It's a revolution that begins by stopping the rush to bed and returning to romance, courtship, necking, and waiting. (This is a purely practical first step if you are the least bit interested in pleasure. Years of clinical observation show that it takes time to build pleasure, intensity, and desire. There is no shortcut to intimacy.) The goal, quite simply, is to change sex from being merely O.K. to being superb — to get away from the old Victorian hangover of shame and to get away from the new impersonal and insensitive performance style of sex — to enjoy the great delight and pleasure of sex and intimacy.

Certain themes recur constantly throughout this book: "slowly," "one step at a time," "gradually," "some people may find," " you might feel." These tentative phrases are partly in recognition of how personal and individual sex is. And these phrases are an accurate description of the way change really happens, slowly, gradually, step by step.

Well, what needs changing? You might begin by looking beyond the physical shapes and functions of lovemaking.

All your life you have been learning your sexual habits and techniques, and your sexual taboos and preferences.

Consider the things that people drag into bed. If thoughts and feelings had physical shapes, you'd see most couples climbing into bed with monsters of guilt, accounting books for keeping score, chains of habit, harpies of anxiety, broken records, faded movies, tangles of apron strings, baggage belonging to long-gone lovers, ghosts from childhood, prohibitions from their fathers, and a murmuring chorus of friends and relations.

Sexual confidence is leaving those distractions outside the bedroom door.

Sexual confidence is being able to talk and listen and laugh sexually, to share dreams and fantasies. It's being able to say what you're scared of and what hurts, and asking for what you want.

Sexual confidence is taking the risk of being vulnerable, childlike, and primitive.

Sexual confidence is being certain of your own needs and strengths. It is knowing how to give and to share — knowing how to create friendship and intimacy. And it is knowing how to deal with sexual problems.

Sexual confidence is knowing that sex isn't only skyrockets at night and emotional earthquakes; it's also playful, wild, awkward, fun, experimental, uncertain, and incidental, a part of the unpredictable life between two people who take all the time it takes to know and care for each other.

Sexual confidence is freedom from anxiety and freedom from the pressures of performance.

Sexual confidence is feeling good about your size and shape, being glad you are who you are. Sexual confidence is feeling good about feeling good.

Sexual confidence is a man, living with a woman for years, making her feel new again. It's a woman throwing the ghost of her mother out of the bedroom; it's a woman teaching a man the ways she likes his tongue to move. Sexual confidence is having the self-assurance and self-worth to try out an outrageous fantasy, and to laugh if it doesn't work.

Learning sexual confidence is a three-stage process. First you need to unlearn the anxieties and other excess freight you may be dragging into bed with you — unlearn the things that prevent you from feeling intense pleasure. Next there are strengths, skills, and techniques to learn and develop. And finally, there is sharing what you have learned, experimenting and exploring the far reaches of your own sexual frontiers.

The point of all this isn't just better sex, although that is a large, happy part of it. It is also this: as you begin to explore and develop sexual potential you didn't realize you had, as you learn to feel comfortable and right about your own sexuality, you are apt to find a new richness of intimacy and communication. The point is to make sex joyful instead of a duty, to make sex loving instead of performing, an occasion for making love instead of just having sex. The point is to replace shame, anxiety, and mediocre sex with beauty, pleasure, and laughter.

I've spent most of my professional life studying sex, and I am happy to report that the more we learn about it, the more we realize that it is an unlimited phenomenon, as vast and unknowable as outer space. But most people barely glimpse the magic and the unknown. Let me list the reasons why: anxiety, guilt, a lack of physical and emotional awareness, a lack of communication, inability to laugh in sex, sexual myths and social pressures, and an emphasis on performance. As you see, it's not a very long list. And you will have, with the techniques that follow, the means to remove those barriers and to become sexually confident.

Sexual Confidence is based on behavior therapy. That is to say, it is not conjecture or one person's opinion, but rather the result of countless observations by numerous scientists. Lest you fear the cold, impersonal stare of science on so emotional a subject as sex, let me hasten to add that sex is indeed full of mystery, and vague, unmeasurable qualities that can be described only imperfectly as desire, joy, and love. And the point of increasing your knowledge about sex is to give you the best possible vantage point for your own discoveries and adventures.

PART ONE

UNLEARNING

Guilt keeps you from being earthy and primitive. You can't jump for joy and howl and writhe with pleasure if you feel guilty.

It has taken you a lifetime to accumulate all of your sexual habits and attitudes. Some you may want to keep. Some you may want to lose. But you can't just wish away guilt or anxiety, and you can't simply forget the sexual myths you've always believed in. The first steps toward acquiring sexual confidence are a kind of spring cleaning — clearing away destructive and obstructive feelings, habits, and misinformation. These first steps aren't always easy ones to take. But they are essential if you want to experience all of the depth and the beauty that is possible.

2

Unlearning Sexual Myths

At first they thought it was just a coincidence — the kind of coincidence you expect to happen at a penthouse cocktail party in New York City. As a waiter passed holding a tray of champagne glasses, they both reached for the same glass. They hadn't even noticed each other. He was young and single. She was young and single. Their hands touched on the glass of champagne, their eyes met, and they fell in love. Later they decided it wasn't a coincidence, it was fate. They had everything in common. They both loved the theater and the ballet, weekends in Vermont, late-night movies on TV, strawberries Romanov, and they both believed in all the sexual myths in America.

She believed men should be big and strong (he was). He believed women should be small and slight (she was). And they both believed in love at first sight, and that if you fell in love you should make love the very first night.

He was Todd and she was Samantha. They were both pleased to see that they each had gaps between their two front teeth, signifying, according to the myth, big sexual appetites. Todd ate several oysters to increase his virility. Samantha wolfed down big black olives in the equally mistaken belief that they would make her more amorous. Then they settled down together in a cozy corner of the party to stare longingly into each other's eyes and drink an entire bottle of champagne.

Let's leave Todd and Samantha staring into each other's eyes and drinking. We'll come back and follow them into bed. But while they are working up the courage to say "Your place or mine?" let's look at this peculiar phenomenon of sexual mythology. Why is there so much of it?

Sexual myth is born in ignorance. When you were young, and believed toads caused warts, sex was rumored to be more important than the moon. But it seemed just as far away. And while some of the older kids bragged about moon landings ("I touched her —— in study hall." "Philippa went all the way"), what it was precisely, how it was done, and what it felt like could only be guessed at. It was a subject for wild speculation. One kid would overhear something and pass a garbled version on to you ("Miss Gompers, the math teacher, got scared when Mr. Truman, the coach, put his thing in her and they had to go to the hospital to get unstuck").

Childish myths are usually so distorted they are easy to spot. We grow up and common sense and experience teach us that penises don't get stuck in vaginas, and that your hand doesn't fall off if you masturbate.

Adult sexual myths are less fantastic and more common. But they, too, flourish in mystery and ignorance. Sexual myths are signs pointing in the wrong direction. They lead you into playing roles fit for the silver screen but not for real life. Movie, television, and magazine heroes and heroines live in two dimensions. A famous face wins the heart of another famous face in a Hollywood blockbuster, and all across the country there are people who really believe that the way to get a woman is to act strong and not say much. Or the way to get a man is to give him everything. Magazine sexual-advice columns (often answering pseudo-letters written by the magazine) say that *this* will turn him on and *that,* done just right, is guaranteed to turn her on.

Ignorance is not bliss. Even experience can be a misleading

teacher. People tend to repeat their sexual mistakes. Real mystery, romance and pleasure, and surprising spontaneous discoveries come not from ignorance but from knowledge — knowing what is true and what is not, knowing yourself and your partner.

But let's be specific. Todd and Samantha have thanked their hostess and left the party. They are in the back seat of a taxi, headed for his place, their hopes up and their desires high.

Myth 1: Cinderella. Samantha has been longing for a prince, a dashing young man who will ride off into big adventures during the day and tuck her into bed and tell her bedtime stories in the evening. Someone strong who will take her life in his hands and make the important decisions and take out the garbage. Todd has been looking for the perfect woman, a lusty lady who will always be young and beautiful and handy with a Cuisinart.

It may seem cold-hearted to throw a bucket of cold water on Cinderella so early in the evening. After all, love is blind. And love has magical power to cure your ills and make you strong. And yes, the first rush of romance is a beautiful, exhilarating high. There is nothing else remotely like it. But the Cinderella myth — that you will go on feeling like a prince and a princess happily ever after — is a cruel deception. It leaves you unprepared for the reality of life together.

Of course nobody's perfect. Only lovers could think so. But beyond the foibles, weaknesses, and infuriating little habits that emerge as the bliss fades, there is another especially important point. There is no one perfect person for you, no one who will fulfill all your dreams and needs. It's unfair to put that burden on anybody's shoulders, especially someone you love. There are dreams that will go unfulfilled. Satisfactions that you will have to find elsewhere. And a great deal you will have to do for yourself.

Moreover, the romance will fade. There's a good deal you can do to make it last. You can almost always create romantic moments. But the huge, overwhelming excitement and joy of first-time romance doesn't last for anybody. Couples believe that other couples are passionately in love, that it's just themselves who've lost the fire. In one recent survey, most couples said that the romance lasted a week, a month, a year, or even two. A very few, who did not live together, said that the intense, obsessive elation of romance lasted for as long as five years. But that was the exception. The Cinderella myth is cruel because it leads people to believe that once the early peak of romance is over, so is the relationship. And so they split up and start looking, once again, for a new prince or princess.

Todd and Samantha have been looking for the perfect partner for years. Chances are, years from now, they will still be looking. That's sad, not just because theirs is a futile, disappointing search, but also because they will miss out on so much. They will miss out on the dignity and the intimacy of a long-term relationship. They will miss the sharing of disasters that time turns into brave, hilarious exploits. They will miss the history of adventures together that give a relationship depth and savor. They will miss the intimacy of a loving friendship, sharing and caring, building a life with another person. Because belief in the Cinderella myth dooms a relationship to an early death — to letdowns, disappointment, and divorce.

On the other hand, there is no law that says a relationship has to last forever to be terrific. Certainly for the moment, Todd and Samantha have no such worries. As the taxi winds through Central Park on the way to Todd's apartment, they are kissing each other passionately. Samantha's tongue is wriggling inside Todd's mouth. Todd has just slipped his hand inside Samantha's blouse. His big hand cups her brassiere and breast. The pleasant warmth, the soft, cushy feeling, the thumping of Samantha's heart, the texture of her nipple, are all distant signals, way off in his hand: for at the moment Todd's mind is churning furiously with a problem closer to home. He doesn't have an erection.

Myth 2: The All-time Stud. Todd is trying to urge his penis into life. "Come on, big fella, don't let me down now. Come on, nothing to be afraid of. Sit up and take notice. It's almost bedtime. Please don't let me down now." Todd recognizes the feeling, and it scares him: the quiet, still, numb feeling that no coaxing will change. Todd firmly believes a young, American male ought to be able to summon up an erection at will. And kissing a passionate, sexy woman, with his hand on her breast, means that his penis should be throbbing, not lolling around like some lazy dog's tongue. Samantha puts her hand on the inside of his thigh. "Good grief, still nothing!" Was the "big fella" going to let him in for the big letdown?

Todd has drunk too much. He has had a long, exhausting, and frustrating day at the office. He doesn't really know the person whose breast he cups. All things have their time and tide and season. But none of these entirely valid reasons would still Todd's fears. It's not so much the absence of the erection per se that scares him, but the humiliation. Even if Samantha was "understanding," his nonerection would mean he didn't live up to the myth of a man being able to have intercourse at any time and any place, no matter what.

The implications of this myth are that men are insensitive. That their sexuality is a reflex reaction. The myth leads men to ignore their exquisite sensitivity. Todd's hand is full of magnificent news that he is ignoring. There are headlines: "NIPPLE RISES TO MEET TODD'S PALM." News stories: "This evening, when for the first time, handsome young Todd slipped his hand inside the beautiful Samantha's blouse, he discovered she wore an acrylic brassiere, B cup, and that she had nipples like pink thimbles." Romantic commentary: "Her heart was pounding. Did this mean that she loved him, too?" Thoughtful editorials: "The smooth texture of the skin about the cup of the bra made young Todd speculate on her heritage, her past, the family fortunes hidden in castle cellars awaiting her betrothal."

Men are endowed with amazing sensitivity. The mere brush against a shoulder or a breast is full of sensations to enjoy.

But Todd's mind was elsewhere. An old, horrible suspicion had risen up from the back of his mind to haunt him. What if the reason he didn't have an erection was that he was sick . . . what if he was, underneath it all, a homosexual?

Myth 3: It's Sick to Be a Homosexual. Homosexuality is a form of sexual expression. There is no reputable current evidence to support the myth that homosexuality is a mental or physical disorder.

The myth grew out of the fact that years ago, when the first serious studies of homosexuals were done, the only people who were studied were in deep emotional pain, in therapy. Freud reported that homosexuals were mentally troubled because he was reporting on his own patients. Had he done the same study on his heterosexual patients, he would have had to reach the same conclusion — that heterosexuals are deeply troubled people. (As for homosexuals being child molesters, as Todd and others believe, a Kinsey Institute study of sexual offenders shows that ninety-seven per cent of child molesters are heterosexuals.)

Homosexuality is not an "aberration" or "perversion"; it is the way some people are. According to a 1948 Kinsey study, thirty-seven per cent of all men have had at least one homosexual experience to orgasm, and fifty per cent have had at least one homosexual experience or fantasy to orgasm. In another Kinsey study, the same figures for women were respectively thirteen and twenty-eight per cent. Since most people are reluctant to discuss homosexual fantasies or experiences, and since the world of 1948 was generally closed to homosexuals, one might safely assume that those figures are conservative.

We do not know why some people have one sexual preference and others another. And we know that we are all creatures of mixed male and female traits. As one lovely young woman put it, "I guess we're all some of one and some of another. It's just which way you happen to tilt."

In fact, if Todd could simply stop worrying about his erection and focus on the sensations in his hand, and on his thigh, where Samantha has rested her elegantly manicured hand, his penis would probably begin to assert a will of its own.

But Samantha has paused, because she has fears of her own. His hand is on her breast. It's stopped. It's not moving. His hand is just, clunk, frozen there. Oh, she thinks, he must be so disappointed.

Myth 4: The Dinosaur Theory. Samantha has always felt insecure about her breasts. They took forever to develop when she was a teen-ager. And they never really grew to star size. Happily, fashions have changed to take some of the wind out of this inflated myth that, like dinosaurs, the biggest breasts are the best.

Now, any number of fashion models and film and TV stars have small breasts. Breast-size fashions change and will no doubt continue to do so. Your breasts aren't fashionable, unfashionable, sexy, or unsexy, they are you. Many men feel some tidal urge toward breasts from birth on throughout their lives. But size plays a role only insofar as some men state a preference for small breasts or large, and insofar as some women long for another size.

Todd was happy enough with the size of Samantha's breasts. It was the size of his penis that continued to preoccupy him. "Come on, dammit, come on!" He, too, believed in the old "bigger is better" dinosaur theory, but he applied it to his own penis. A few facts here should suffice. While the male penis may vary in size in its flaccid state, there is far *less* variation in erect-penis size. There is no known study of female preference about penis size. It seems to be a nonissue among most women. Todd felt that his penis was somewhat above average size, and he felt somewhat superior because of it. Except, of course, when it would not get hard.

Perhaps this was a taste of the future. Todd had felt for some time that he had better get all the sex he could now.

Because, as everybody knows, when you get old you can't. Now at thirty-three, maybe this was a sign that his sexual days would soon be over.

Myth 5: Senior Citizens Can't. Oh yes they can. As Shakespeare said, "My age is as a lusty winter." You can be sexual at ninety. The key is to remain sexually active. As Paul Goodman said, "The more you do, the more you can."

Advancing age doesn't leave you unchanged, but there are compensations. Starting at age eighteen, the male refractory period (the phase following ejaculation, during which the male is unlikely to have an erection and unable to have an orgasm) begins to lengthen. At eighteen it might last for five seconds or an hour. At ninety it may be a day or a week before a man will have an erection again. With age, the erection becomes less firm and ejaculation is less powerful. It may take a man longer to get an erection, and he may need more direct stimulation. On the other hand, an older man is able to last much longer, and that can mean he will be more in tune with a woman's longer time to orgasm.

And women, as they get older, often find their sex drive goes up, not down. There are some significant changes with menopause: less lubrication, less elasticity of the vaginal walls. These conditions, however, can be treated quite easily by a gynecologist.

With women's desire rising, and men's endurance lengthening, sex in your sixties, seventies, eighties, and nineties can be very good indeed.

Once Todd and Samantha were in Todd's apartment, high over the city streets, with a view of the East River, Todd stopped worrying about being old and being gay. He was on home ground now, and he had a role to play. He turned the lights down low, put on some soft classical guitar music, and poured "very superior old pale champagne" brandy into two balloon brandy snifters — just to make sure everything went sexually smoothly.

Myth 6: Alcohol Is Good for Sex. All alcohol, whether it's fine cognac or beer, is a depressant. It lowers reaction times, numbs sensations, and in large quantities causes severe nausea and unconsciousness. Todd and Samantha weren't feeling nauseated, but after drinking the champagne all of their senses were somewhat dulled, along with their judgment.

In small doses — a drink or two, or a little wine — alcohol may relax you and tend to lower your inhibitions. In larger doses, it is the single most important cause of the male's loss of his erection. The more you drink, the more you can't. Clinical evidence suggests that over time, heavy alcohol consumption causes irreversible damage to the liver, and to the male sexual response.

But now Todd's penis was beginning to struggle against the lethargy of alcohol. Samantha looked so pretty in the soft light. He led her over to the picture window. Todd had done this many times before and he knew what to do. With his arm around Samantha, looking over the city lights, the jetliners slowly rising and falling on the horizon, he began to talk about his cabin in the woods.

Myth 7: The Male Burden. The image of a cabin somewhere, leafy, green, simple, and pure, beyond the city lights, was almost irresistible for Samantha. She hardly noticed Todd's hand unbuttoning the back of her blouse while he spoke. But when he began to unbutton her skirt, followed by the zipper's quiet rasp, she began to feel uneasy. What was happening here? Yes, she did want to make love with this big, handsome man, but things were going a little too quickly for her. Still, she didn't want to seem prim or old-fashioned. She looked up questioningly into Todd's eyes. He sank to his knees in front of her, tugging down her skirt, slip, and panties so they lay in a bunched-up heap on the floor. She felt pasty white and exposed in front of the big picture window. Then Todd was putting his tongue into her navel.

The myth of the man as the grand orchestrator of a sexual

symphony, with the woman as the passive instrument, has its drawbacks. It creates anxiety for the woman. For she truly is "out of control" of the situation, not knowing what's going to happen next, or indeed, how long this particular stage of the orchestration will go on. It's frustrating, because she doesn't make known her desires and fears, pleasures and discomforts. She bears them silently. For the man it's an impossible task, founded on guesswork (now she's ready for . . .) or a previous agenda or both. It's a kind of denial of the woman's creativity and sexuality.

Samantha realized Todd was tugging at her shoes. Todd was on his hands and knees now, bending over her feet. Her shoes had tiny buckles on the straps on the side and he was having trouble unbuckling them. Should she bend down and help him? she wondered. No, he was in charge. He knew what he was doing. Standing in a pool of her rumpled clothing, with Todd struggling at her shoes, she felt a shoe strap break.

Todd stood up, grinning uncertainly. She smiled back, a little worried. What was going to happen next? Todd took her hand and gave her a little tug toward the bedroom. Naked below the waist, her brassiere and blouse flapping loosely, still holding the balloon brandy glass, she followed him. "Well," she thought, "just go with the flow. Let it happen naturally. Just let go and it'll all happen O.K."

Myth 8: Lovemaking Happens Naturally. Once they were in the bedroom, Todd led Samantha to the bed and she sat down. He stood in front of her and took off his jacket and tie, his shirt and trousers. Samantha guessed it was time to take off her blouse and brassiere. Setting her brandy glass on the floor she did so, feeling very naked, worried that her breasts were too small, her tummy too fat. Todd kicked his shoes off and sent the balloon brandy snifter rolling across the carpet, spilling a trail of brandy. Samantha stood up, thinking she would find a towel to clean it up. Todd pulled back the covers and pushed her gently back down on the bed. "Don't worry about it," he said. She worried about it. What if they stepped on the glass in the dark? Evidently his erection had returned. Samantha lay back on the black sheets. "Don't worry about anything," she repeated to herself. "Just let go and it'll all happen naturally."

It's true that sexual feelings are natural, but lovemaking has to be learned. For those who would ask "How do animals copulate if not naturally?" I would point out that the higher animals learn copulation by watching, something we humans rarely have the chance to do. The lower the animal, the more instinct is involved; the higher the animal the more learning is involved. It has been shown that monkeys isolated from other monkeys are completely inept at intercourse. They don't know how because they never had the chance to learn how.

The myth that lovemaking comes naturally also implies that it is unromantic to say you don't know how to do this, or to show and teach someone how to do something. It's too clinical and calculating, says the myth. And yet asking questions, being open about your uncertainty, explaining, and teaching can be a warm and intimate part of lovemaking.

Samantha was feeling anything but warm and intimate. For Todd had climbed into bed with her, had whispered a few words in her ear ("Just imagine you're up in the cabin in Vermont, the wind blowing through the trees"), and then crouched down between her legs and buried his head there.

Myth 9: The Sure-fire Erogenous Zones. In the backs of their minds, along with the other mythological clutter, both Todd and Samantha have erogenous maps of the human body. The pelvic region and the female breasts are colored bright red, and the rest of the body is colored a kind of dull gray, as if all sexuality were centered in a few "hot" areas. To be sure, these are sensitive areas, but the feet and neck, thighs and arms, scalp, mouth, spine, tongue, hands, stomach, and ears can be erotic, too. Pleasure is where you find it, and your body is richly endowed with centers of pleasure. Moreover, a genital touch may or may not feel sexual. It may feel shocking or dull. There are no push-button turn-ons in sex.

Todd is vigorously rubbing his tongue down and up Samantha's vaginal lips. He takes care to give her clitoris, at the top of her vaginal lips, some extra-firm licks. He has no way of knowing that Samantha finds his tongue rough and harsh, or that she would much prefer indirect stimulation and a much lighter touch, because he won't ask. And she won't tell him. Todd believes that being a little rough turns women on. It's part of his belief that, underneath it all, women are sexually all alike.

Myth 10: When She Lubricates, She's Ready. Todd could not help noticing that Samantha was beginning to lubricate. He believed that meant she was ready for intercourse, the goal he had been seeking.

The truth is that lubrication is the *first* sign of sexual excitement in a woman. It means she has just begun to become excited. When a woman is highly aroused the uterus lifts up from the vaginal barrel and the vaginal walls expand to make room for a penis. At that point she may be ready for intercourse. There is no way for a man to tell this with any certainty. He has to rely on his partner's judgment.

According to Kinsey, about half of American couples have three to ten minutes of foreplay before intercourse. That figure should be contrasted with recent clinical evidence that suggests that many women need fourteen minutes or more of clitoral stimulation for an orgasm. Todd had buried his head between Samantha's legs for 3.5 minutes now, and it was time, he guessed, for intercourse. And so, his penis in his hand, he rose up and bent forward, supporting himself on his left elbow, and pushing this way and that he entered her.

Myth 11: The "Normal" Position. As Todd began thrusting, Samantha put her legs around his and moved with him, searching his eyes for love. "Oh, oh, oh," he said. "Oh, oh, oh," she said.

There is nothing wrong with the "missionary" position. (Christian missionaries taught the South Sea Islanders that it is "normal" for the man to be on top and the woman to lie on her back.) It's especially good for male excitement. Thrusting is the deepest and muscle tension is the greatest. And it's fine for the female, as long as the male is considerate enough to support his weight on his knees and elbows. But it is by no means the only possibility. A woman often finds that her movement is somewhat restricted in this position, thus decreasing her chances for pleasure. The problem is not so much the position itself, but the belief that it is the *only* position, that other positions are deviations, aberrations, impure, weird, unmanly, or whorish.

There is no "normal" position.

As Todd continued thrusting, Samantha couldn't help wishing she felt more excited. She began to wish she could reach down and touch herself, but that might be a terrible insult to Todd's prowess as a lover. In fact, she thought, if she didn't masturbate so often, she'd probably enjoy this a lot more.

Myth 12: Masturbators Make Second-rate Lovers. We'll cover masturbation in a later chapter on guilt — the reasons masturbation is good for you: it's nonfattening, you don't have to look your best, and so on. And masturbation is the easiest way for women to learn to have orgasms. It can also add to your and your partner's pleasure during lovemaking.

If a woman can masturbate to orgasm, then she is much more likely to have an orgasm during intercourse, particularly if she stimulates herself during intercourse or shows her partner how to touch her clitoris during intercourse.

But what is troubling Samantha now is guilt. Guilt about masturbation and guilt because she feels she should be more excited. She feels miles away from an orgasm, but she'd like to have one "for his sake." Her dilemma is that if she touched herself, she probably would have an orgasm. But that would be wrong, she thinks. The right way to have an orgasm is with a man deep in your vagina.

Myth 13: The Right and Wrong Kind of Female Orgasm. "After all," Samantha thinks as Todd plunges from side to side, "a vaginal orgasm is so much deeper and so much more meaningful and satisfying than a clitoral orgasm."

The culprit behind that particular myth is one of the great mythmakers, Sigmund Freud. He created an arbitrary difference between a clitoral orgasm (inferior) and a vaginal orgasm (healthy, normal), which is ludicrous! If we are going to make that distinction then we should also designate a breast orgasm, a toe orgasm, a fantasy orgasm, an ear-lobe orgasm. Freud should have consulted Mrs. Freud. An orgasm is an all-over body response. There is no such thing as a vaginal orgasm. An orgasm is an orgasm is an orgasm.

In the early 1960s, William Masters and Virginia Johnson measured the physical intensity of female orgasms. They found that the most intense female orgasm, on average, was experienced through masturbation. The next most intense orgasm was through manual or oral stimulation from a partner. And the least intense orgasm was through intercourse.

There are women who would dispute that. Those figures are, after all, only averages. And orgasms come in all sizes, shapes, and forms, from ripples to volcanoes.

What is irritating is the self-proclaimed experts who tell women that there is a certain kind of orgasm they ought to have. In Woody Allen's film *Manhattan,* a forty-year-old woman at a cocktail party says, "After all these years, I finally had an orgasm. And my doctor told me it was the wrong kind." After a short pause for laughter, Woody Allen says, "I never had the wrong kind."

There is no wrong kind of orgasm. Only wrong myths. The intensity of an orgasm is not dependent on whether it is an ear-lobe or intercourse orgasm. It is dependent on several different things: how much stimulation there was beforehand, the mood that night, how intensely you're involved with this person, the last time you had sex. Sometimes orgasms may build, and the second may be stronger than the first, and the third stronger still. The reverse is often true for men, who usually experience a tapering off of intensity if they have more than one orgasm during a round of lovemaking.

The male orgasm is more direct; it is usually faster and easier to get to. The female orgasm is astonishingly complex. In fact, some researchers theorize that only human females have orgasms, that other female animals do not. Certainly female animals give no outward sign. I have seen hundreds of film clips of animals in intercourse. Along with many other researchers, I was unable to see any indication of orgasm in these female animals. Except, perhaps, the cat. The female cat often rolls over after sex. Is she silently enjoying a sublime, feline orgasm? Or simply rolling over? Thus far, she's not talking.

So it may just be that the human-female orgasm is more highly developed, more complicated, more evolved, more easily interrupted, and harder to achieve than the male orgasm.

In any case, in every human-female orgasm certain specific things happen. Blood rushes to the pelvis, muscle tension builds, the clitoris engorges, and, during the orgasm, there are usually vaginal contractions, which may or may not be felt. What needs to be stressed is that the clitoris is the center of sexual excitement for women. Unfortunately, it is placed wrong for intercourse. It may be subject to a certain amount of tugging and shifting, indirectly, from the thrustings of intercourse, but it is well clear of the action. Which means that for women intercourse is the least likely way to experience orgasm. For not only is the clitoris on the sidelines, so to speak, but there are very few nerve endings inside the vagina. Of the women Kinsey studied, eighty-six per cent had little or no sensation inside the vagina.

Added to that, most men (seventy-five per cent), as Kinsey found, have an orgasm within two minutes after penetration. And most women (seventy-five per cent) need more than two minutes of stimulation to achieve orgasm. If, as some clinicians now suggest, many women take fourteen minutes or more to reach orgasm, then we have an average gap of twelve minutes between male and female orgasms, a wide space of time between the end of intercourse, as signaled by the male ejaculation, and the achievement of female orgasm. I should point out, as Kinsey did, that some women have orgasms within seconds. However, most, like Samantha, take considerably longer than their male partners.

Samantha felt her mind beginning to drift. She looked across the pillow out the window, and wondered if this would be a good night to be on the beach, to feel the cool sand and hear the waves. To make love with a man, a stranger she had met by the fireside, to feel him . . . good grief, she felt ashamed. It was so unfair of her — her first time making love with Todd and here she was dreaming up some fantasy about some stranger on a beach. She must be perverted.

Myth 14: Sexual Fantasies Are Perverted. Samantha tried desperately to think of other things. She tried to look into Todd's eyes, but they were closed. He seemed to be getting very excited.

Fantasies are part of being human. They are like daydreaming. Some fantasies are about going to the seashore, some about making love with strangers. Whatever they are, people rarely talk about them. And because there is this conspiracy of silence about sexual fantasies, we grow up thinking that we are the only ones who have them. Many of us are told they are "impure thoughts," that having those thoughts is just the same as acting them out. Poor Samantha, not even halfway through making love with Todd and already she's accusing herself of being unfaithful to him.

Some people fantasize, some don't. The ones who do don't necessarily fall into any one pattern. People fantasize about heterosexual sex, incest, homosexual sex, sadism, masochism, being tied up, rape, harems, friends, movie stars, and centerfolds. Some people have one fantasy, with variations, over and over. Others have lots of different fantasies. I know of no harm in it.

Samantha has suppressed her lover-on-the-beach fantasy and she is looking for a fresh, clean thought to replace it — church perhaps. Or, wait a second, Todd's cabin in Vermont. She tried to picture it. High on a ridge in Vermont.

"Are you coming?"

"What?" Samantha asked.

"Are you coming?" Todd asked again.

"Oh yes, yes, of course." Samantha thought he meant to the cabin.

Myth 15: Simultaneous Orgasm. Todd imagined they came together. He silently congratulated himself on his prowess. He needn't have. It wasn't even close.

Nor need it have been. When you consider the differences in timing and pacing between two people, and the amount of tension and effort it takes to achieve a simultaneous orgasm, one has to ask is it really worth the effort? Moreover, having orgasms at different times allows you to enjoy your partner's orgasm as well as your own.

I don't mean to deny the occasional magnificence of a simultaneous orgasm (like other orgasms, they vary from mild to ecstatic), but like intercourse itself, when you set it up as a goal you diminish the other pleasures and intimacies along the way. You tend to become overly concerned with sexual performance and lose the intimate, loving interchange that makes physical pleasure merely the top wave of the sea changes of sexuality.

When they untangled themselves, Todd held Samantha tenderly in his arms. "Did you use any contraception?" he asked.

Myth 16: Contraception Is the Woman's Responsibility. "Oh no." Samantha said. "Did you?"

While Samantha ran off to the bathroom, Todd rolled over and went to sleep.

Myth 17: Men Lose Interest in a Woman After They Make Love with Her. When Samantha returned from the bathroom, Todd was on his back, snoring loudly. She felt terribly insulted. Was she really so boring? Was that all he wanted her for, sex? Well, maybe her lovemaking wasn't the best in the world. Maybe it was her fault. Next time she would have to try harder to please him.

What Samantha doesn't know is that Todd has entered into the refractory phase of sexual response. After ejaculation, a man's excitement drops off sharply (unlike a woman, who feels a much slower and gradual decline of pleasure). During the refractory phase, which may last from a few seconds to days, an erection may appear, but an orgasm is simply not possible. Very often after the great release and relaxation of an orgasm, a man will feel drowsy. Todd is asleep not because he's insensitive and uncaring; it's just a normal male reaction after orgasm.

Samantha climbed into bed sadly. As Todd snored, Samantha lay wide awake, staring at the ceiling, wondering if the cabin would be worth it.

*

Let us leave them there. They have earned their rest. They have by no means illustrated all the sexual myths in America. There are many, many more. But the myths that Todd and Samantha cling to are among the most common. The confusion and disappointment they feel are a very real experience for a great many people.

Sexual myth is simply prejudice, expecting yourself and others to be people we are not and do things we cannot or should not do.

Sexual confidence means having a clear sense of who you are physically, spiritually, sexually, and emotionally, knowing where the myth leaves off and where you begin.

3

Untying Old Ties

Your mother smiles as she ties her lead weights around your neck with a ribbon. Dad tightens his belt of silent criticism around your waist and says, "It's for your own good." Friends hang their sexual worries on you as if they were doing you a favor.

You carry around other people's sexual fears and prohibitions for all kinds of reasons — reasons such as "it seems to make sense" or "that's what everybody does" — or you may have been carrying certain fears for so long that you feel they are entirely your own. Your sexual attitudes come from so many different directions — from the mass media, religion, teachers, parents, friends, and enemies, perhaps from a phrase overheard on a train — that the origins of sexual attitudes are often obscured.

Wherever they come from, your sexual attitudes aren't necessarily permanent. You can change them. I'd like to give you some techniques for making those changes. Then, if some of your sexual attitudes interfere with your life and your pleasure, you'll know how to change those attitudes to suit yourself.

I am not talking about making a total break with what you have thought and felt in the past. Nor am I talking about trading Victorian inhibitions for the new, equally repressive performance criteria of instant sex and keeping score. It's possible to say good-by to negatives in your past without adopting new ones. But often the feelings you learned in the past conflict with what you want to do now.

Suppose, for example, when you were a baby playing with your toes, amusing your mom, you got bored with that and reached down between your legs to play. Yum, that felt good. Slap, your mother slapped your hand away. That hurt. Later you were scolded. "BAD."

It was your first lesson in shame. Some of your most intense, enduring emotional lessons are your first ones. The shock of having your hand slapped away can reverberate for the rest of your life.

Your feelings are entrenched in long-established patterns. If you want to change them you have to change your present emotional patterns. Happily, interrupting and changing these habits can be a reasonably straightforward process. If you follow techniques such as "thought stopping" and "silent ridicule," described later in this chapter, you can get rid of the shackles and impediments you drag into bed.

Slapping a hand away is a simple example. Usually sexual anxieties and fears are learned more subtly. Possibly there was a conspiracy of silence in your childhood. Sex was one of the intimate subjects your parents and teachers never talked about: sex, you learned, was not to be talked about. Possibly they taught you that sex was only for marriage or for making babies. Perhaps the child they taught wisely and affectionately is a different person now in a different world. Perhaps their lessons no longer apply, and there is no point in remaining tied to them.

Perhaps these lessons from the past are keeping you from something specific that you want to do or to feel. You'd like to be able to feel more relaxed in talking about sex. Or there's someone you'd like to make love with without hearing dusty, moralistic whispers from your conscience. Perhaps you would like to feel easier about having oral sex. Or you'd like to relax about not wanting oral sex. Maybe you'd like to get undressed without feeling foolish. Maybe you'd just like to feel that sex is O.K., that it's good, not dirty.

In no other place can you be so free as when you've closed the door and are alone with someone else, private and intimate. Unfortunately, it's the one place where most people are so unfree — hung up, bound, and weighted down with the fears and shibboleths of generations, from great-grandfather to now.

One particularly clear-cut example of a woman who brought her mother's anxieties to bed with her was Marcia.

MARCIA, THIRTY-FOUR-YEAR-OLD BANKER. Marcia's upbringing was traditionally religious and middle-class. Her parents emphasized that sex was dirty. And only for marriage. She and her husband, Richard, did a lot of "making out" when they were dating. But she resisted the powerful desire to have intercourse, obeying her mother's taboos. And then, two months before her wedding, she and Richard made love in her parents' living room while her parents slept in a bedroom down the hall. What might have been a wonderful first-time experience made her feel terrible. She felt she had violated her parents' trust. And after that, every time she approached sex she thought of her mother's disapproval. In effect, she was bringing her mother into her bedroom.

Marcia's honeymoon was a disaster. Her husband had rented a small fishing shack on the tip of Florida, and they had flown down from the Minnesota winter to lie in the sun, fish, be alone, and make love. Marcia was so put off by lovemaking that she insisted on staying out in the sun and, as a result, got severely burned. She felt lucky. It gave her another excuse for not making love.

When Marcia came to see me she had been married five years. "My husband wants sex all the time," said Marcia. By using one ploy or another, she kept their lovemaking down to once every ten days. She was very much in love with her husband, and he was very much in love with her. And yet she knew that keeping her mother in the bedroom was putting a terrible strain on her marriage.

I used several techniques (which I'll explain later in the chapter) with Marcia: "thought stopping," "ridicule," and "assertive dialogues." The breakthrough, when Marcia finally got her mother to "leave" her bedroom, came when Marcia could enjoy taking Richard's penis in her mouth without imagining that her mother was watching. Marcia enjoys sex with Richard now, and often she initiates their lovemaking. As a bonus, she now finds that she is relaxed instead of upset about her two-year-old son's exploring himself sexually. "It's lovely," she said, "to know that I'm not passing my parents' sexual anxieties on to my son, and to feel so much pleasure in my own sexuality."

As you become aware of your own preferences and boundaries as a sexual person, there are attitudes and anxieties you may wish to modify slightly, change radically, or even erase altogether. In other words, I am suggesting that you do some house cleaning — that you get rid of the impediments that clutter your bed.

Thought Stopping

The easiest and most effective technique for unlearning thoughts that impede your pleasure is called thought stopping. Developed by Dr. Joseph Wolpe, the father of behavior therapy, thought stopping is powerful and easily learned. Thought stopping is specific, direct, active, and positive — qualities that are all typical of behavior therapy. It works by derailing a thought cycle and substituting a rewarding, pleasurable thought for the one you'd like to stop.

Why thought stopping works is a little more complex. On a very basic level, many neurons in your nervous system have a double link. One link excites an action or emotion, another link inhibits other actions or emotions. In physical terms, for example, the neurons that order your smile muscles to tighten also, at the same time, inhibit your frown muscles from tightening. Wolpe has shown that this double link of action/inhibition also exists emotionally. Love inhibits hate. Laughter is inhibited by sadness, anger, or anxiety. And laughter, in turn, can inhibit sadness, anger, and anxiety.

In other words, the unlearning that you do with thought stopping is more than rationally deciding to stop thinking a certain destructive thought. It is also emotionally countering that thought, and it is emotionally unlearning that thought. Here's how it works: The instant an unwelcome guilt- or anxiety-producing thought occurs ("Oh, what would mother think" or "I'm not supposed to touch myself" or "I'm not supposed to enjoy this" or "This is just for reproduction"), shout "STOP" as loudly as you can, slam your hand down, and replace that thought with a gorgeous, delicious thought.

Since slamming your hand down and screaming "STOP" is apt to make your partner leap up and run away, let me add a few footnotes here. First, you need to practice alone until you've mastered the technique. Next, you will need a short list of thoughts to replace the ones you want to get rid of. Then, you need shout out loud only the first few times you practice thought stopping on your own; later, when you are with someone, you can "shout" "STOP" to yourself, silently. Finally, the technique demands practice.

So make a list of pleasurable thoughts. You don't have to make a long list. You are free to come up with the wildest, craziest or mildest, tamest thoughts you like. The thoughts are yours alone and nobody else need ever know them. The idea is to have a thought that is interesting enough to engage your attention for a while, and pleasurable enough to reward you for stopping the old thought.

Let me give you some examples of thought-stopping

thoughts. You are free to use any you choose. Or you may prefer to use your own.

AUDREY, TWENTY-EIGHT-YEAR-OLD ASSISTANT PROFESSOR OF HISTORY. Audrey often worried about what her father would think about her making love with a Catholic. To stop this repetitive, self-defeating thought chain, she used the following thoughts.

AUDREY'S LIST

1. Ralph finally asks her to marry him. She happily turns him down.

2. She loses ten pounds.

3. The woman in clogs in the overhead apartment goes away on vacation forever.

KEN, TWENTY-YEAR-OLD COLLEGE STUDENT. Ken was in the habit of dragging an old image of his high-school sweetheart into bed with him. In the image, his former sweetheart was absolutely perfect in every way. So his present lover not only had to share Ken with a "perfect" rival, she also had to endure the indignity of being compared with a centerfold saint. Of course his present lover didn't know Ken was thinking about his high-school sweetheart and comparing this former lover with her. But Ken did. And he knew it was complicating and inhibiting their lovemaking. Here are some of the thoughts he used to stop thoughts of his former lover.

KEN'S LIST

1. In a short, powerful speech to the U.N. (later rebroadcast on the seven-o'clock news), Ken persuades the delegates to take the first steps toward what is destined to become a peaceful world.

2. Suddenly, fast-food restaurants are outlawed.

3. He is lying naked on a South Pacific beach with sand as fine as powder. His legs are lapped by the water. As he raises his head, a young woman who has been diving for pearls comes out of the sea to lie between his legs and then slides down to take his penis in her mouth. The cold water drops from her hair, sending shocks across his hot skin.

HARVEY, FORTY-EIGHT-YEAR-OLD TAX LAWYER. Harvey's parents were divorced. His father's early warnings, when Harvey was a child, never let him forget what dangerous betrayers women are. To stop his father's distracting, irrelevant warnings, Harvey used the following scenes:

HARVEY'S LIST

1. On the teak deck of a fifty-foot mahogany sailboat headed for Crete, a nude deck hand smiles as she pours champagne all over Harvey's body.
2. A wealthy eccentric uncle, of whom Harvey had never heard before, has willed Harvey his pristine two-toned 1933 Duesenberg SJ boat-tailed speedster. The two-seater car, now worth around a quarter of a million dollars, was driven only on summer afternoons to Westchester country clubs in 1933, '34, and '35. It has 800 miles on the odometer. Harvey starts it up, hears the whine of the supercharger, lets out the clutch, and drives at full speed around the Indy 500 track, sliding sideways through turn one.

As you can see, some people become very involved in the details of their "thought stoppers." Others find simple thoughts effective.

INGRID, TWENTY-NINE-YEAR-OLD DIVORCED MOTHER OF THREE. Ingrid's best friend urged her to celebrate her freedom by "sleeping around." Ingrid didn't want casual sex. She kept her friend's insistent advice out of her mind with the following thoughts:

INGRID'S LIST

1. She moves into a self-cleaning house.
2. She writes poetry and is published in *The New Yorker*.
3. The first daffodil of spring blooming in slow motion. The fragrance of the flower, its sunrise color, and the sound of bird songs in the woods.

CARY, THIRTY-SIX-YEAR-OLD COMPUTER ANALYST. Cary's childhood priest lived on in his memory, warning him of the dangers of "earthly pleasures." Cary silenced the distracting admonitions with these scenes:

CARY'S LIST

1. He is on horseback in Montana. The sun is dropping behind the mountains, taking with it the last warmth of the day. Across the plain, in the far distance, he can just see the campfire by the river. He has six miles to ride.
2. His wife when he first saw her, in high-school study hall, in a sweater and short skirt, biting on a pencil, trying to understand calculus.
3. Key West sunset.
4. Hang-gliding in the Rockies.

So first find a thought, powerful and intriguing enough to stop the negative thought — to stop you from repeating a deeply ingrained thought pattern. Find a quiet place and time to practice. Then, on purpose, bring on the negative thought. The instant the negative thought enters your mind, shout "STOP" and replace that thought with your thought stopper. Practice thought stopping at least ten times once a day and do it whenever the negative thought occurs to you throughout the day. Within a week, you probably won't need to shout "STOP." While slamming your hand down is helpful, even necessary at first, you will find with practice that snapping a rubber band around your wrist or digging a finger into your palm will work for you. And with a few days' practice, you will be able to simply "shout" "STOP" silently to yourself to stop the thought. That way, when the negative thought tries to interfere with your lovemaking you can stop the negative thought silently and instantly.

Thought stopping is a simple, powerful technique. On the other hand, the negative thoughts that you'd like to stop are apt to be deeply entrenched in your mind. The first time or the first ten times you shout "STOP," pound the desk, and bring on another thought, the negative thought may not stay away. The negative thought may have been going through your mind for years, digging in deeper and deeper. So thought stopping takes daily practice. Your thought-stopping thoughts are new and not so strong as the old negative thoughts. But with setting aside five minutes for practice a day, plus using thought stopping whenever the negative thought occurs to you, you should notice the negative thought losing its hold on you within a week or two.

Silent Ridicule

Breaking the chains to your past — clearing the distractions from your mind — coming to bed without dragging childhood taboos and former lovers with you: the first step (a sort of psychic house cleaning) is primarily thought stopping. But thought stopping alone may not be enough to dislodge a strong authoritarian figure. Not all of us are saddled with one (a father who was always right, a mother who was always telling you you were wrong), but if you find a negative dominant figure from your past who still bothers you, there is an ex-

cellent way to evict their put-downs, prohibitions, moraliz-
ings, and mushy sanctity.

HELEN, FORTY-FOUR-YEAR-OLD NURSE. Helen's father was a
judge. Loquacious, articulate, self-confident, he used to say he
"loved to hear a smart man talk." He was, in his opinion, never
wrong. A strong moralist, he drummed his moral code into
Helen when she was a young girl. "He was pretty drastic,"
Helen said. "He really felt women should be seen and not
heard. Sex, of course was a forbidden subject. But I was given
a clear understanding that for women, sex was not to be enjoyed as well as not talked about." Helen married at eighteen,
raised a family, and separated from her husband two years
ago. Now that she is on her own, she'd like to enjoy her freedom. But she finds that, although her father died many years
ago, she still feels his strong disapproval when she goes to bed
with a man or even thinks about it.

But now, when she feels her father's disapproval, Helen
imagines him as an old-fashioned New England Puritan, holding a large Bible and shaking his fist, so now she can see his
moralizing as a relic from her past. More important, by ridi-
culing the moralizing she's able to separate that trait from her
father, whom she now views more realistically, not as a dominating authority figure to be feared, but as a man and a father
who loved her. Most important, she's able to feel free from his
values and comfortable with her own.

The technique of imagining someone in a ridiculous situation or outfit is called silent ridicule. It's especially effective
in taking the pedestal out from under the authorities of your
past when they interfere with your living in the present. When
you feel their criticism or disapproval interfering with your
love life, imagine them in a ridiculous or absurd scene.

The secret of silent ridicule is to find a situation or background or gesture that makes the person ridiculous by emphasizing a flaw in that person's personality. And the trick is to

make that person seem ridiculous without arousing your pity. You want to revoke that person's authority in your sex life, not feel sorry for him or her.

Here are a few more examples of silent ridicule.

MARY ANNE, NINETEEN-YEAR-OLD COLLEGE STUDENT. Mary Anne had a very strong, dominating mother, who was constantly criticizing her. Nothing Mary Anne ever did was good enough for her. Mary Anne found her mother's imagined criticism especially upsetting in the bedroom. She was able to stop imagining her mother's haranguing ("For heaven's sake, you little milquetoast, he's not very attractive. Is he the best you can get?") by imagining her mother in a red, white, and blue superwoman suit, complete with a cape and tights and a big *S* on her bosom.

KATHY, TWENTY-FOUR-YEAR-OLD STEWARDESS. Kathy's mother wanted her to stay home in Texas, raise a family, and join the local social circle. She pictured Kathy's being an airline stewardess as one step away from being a prostitute. When Kathy went to bed with a man and felt her mother's horrified disapproval, she pictured her mother as a donkey, shaking her head. As Kathy said, "My mother is really a kind, generous person, and I love her. But that doesn't give her the right to stick her nose into my private life."

One man pictures his stern father in a candy-striped pinafore. Another, whose father disapproves of his being in love with a man, pictures his father riding a hobbyhorse. Another man, whose father beat him for masturbating, pictures his father masturbating in a porno movie house; strong medicine, perhaps, but it works for that person. One woman, whose mother disapproves of her living with a married man, pictures her mother in a Minnie Mouse outfit, complete with a big bow and funny shoes. Another woman pictures her mother as a statue in a public park.

Lest these seem cruel and unusual punishments, think for a moment how cruel it is for the images and attitudes of another era to keep pleasure out of your life now.

Assertive Dialogues

1. Get Out of Here, Father Dear

Silent ridicule puts those muggers of your emotions and thieves of your pleasures in perspective. But not everyone is able to find the perfect silent-ridicule scene. You may honor and respect your parents too much, you may feel uneasy putting authoritarian figures in funny hats and diapers, or you may just not want to imagine a silly scene. In that case, you can use a dialogue in your imagination to help you stand up for yourself when bullied by an emotional intruder. Your mother, for example, makes a dramatic entrance at a crucial moment, waving a guilty conscience at the back of your mind. Greet her: "Hi, Mom. Interesting you should show up just as I'm about to have oral sex. Listen, I'm busy now. Come back when I'm doing dishes." "Well, hello, Mother. I can't talk with Tom's tongue in my mouth." "Hey, Dad, imagine seeing you here. Could you leave for a while. I really appreciate all the trouble you went to just to jump into my mind while I'm lying on top of Dave. We'll talk later. Maybe in a year."

The dialogue serves two purposes. First, it puts you in charge of that imaginary figure who keeps intruding when you want to be sexual with someone; you can feel your independence as you turn the figure around and send him or her away. And it keeps you from being defensive. The dialogue is based on one of the tenets of behavior therapy, as discovered by Dr. Joseph Wolpe: assertive behavior reduces anxiety. So by all means assert yourself with mental intruders. It will make you feel better. "Oh, hello, Mother. I didn't hear you knock. I don't think you've met Harry. I'll introduce you as soon as I let him up. In the meantime, close the door quietly when you leave." "COACH! What an amazing surprise finding you here, just as Frank is kissing me on the neck. Why don't you go draw up some new plays and I'll see you next football season."

2. Conversations in the Back of Your Head

There are two more dialogue techniques that are closely related to the one above. Manuel Smith, in his book *I Feel Guilty When I Say No,* calls them "fogging" and "broken record." You can agree with everything the mommies and daddies of your conscience say (fogging), as long as you stick to your point (broken record). Here, from my files, are some examples:

MOM: You're not married to this person.

YOU: No. That's right.

MOM: You shouldn't have sex with this person.

YOU: Right. You sure have a point there. A lot of folks say it's wrong. But I want to be sexual with Tom.

MOM: You could get hurt.

YOU: Yes. I'm taking risks. But I've really been looking forward to having sex with Tom.

MOM: He only wants you for sex.

YOU: You may be right. But I want sex, too.

Agreeing with those mind ghosts and emotional vampires not only throws them off balance (they are used to your running away and hiding when they show up), it keeps you from being defensive while sticking to your point. And it's reassuring and strengthening to hear yourself stand up for yourself.

DAD: That's not the sort of girl your mother would approve of.

YOU: That's right. Mom probably wouldn't approve. I sure do like Marie.

DAD: You have to realize you have very different back-
        grounds.

YOU: Sure do. Different is what she is. She's wonderful.

DAD: You never know with these people.

YOU: No, you never know. Keeps you alert. Marie's great.

DAD: I don't think you should let your sexual desires cloud
        your judgment.

YOU: Right, I sure don't want to be clouded with sexual de-
        sires. I sure do like Marie.

DAD: That's a disgusting thing you're doing with her.

YOU: It's really disgusting, all right. Yum. Marie's just fine.

Sometimes it's even more difficult to stand up to friends.
Apart from saying good-by to the ghosts and negatives haunt-
ing your past, you are also living in the present. And of the
demons who clutter your bed, none babble louder than those
we call social pressures, fashion, or "what everybody is doing."

LAUREN, EIGHTEEN-YEAR-OLD COLLEGE FRESHMAN. "Every
magazine I open *assumes* that I'm having sex. Well, I think
sex should be saved for being in love, probably even marriage.
It's really a drag having to go through this struggle on every
date. 'Oh, Lauren,' my dates say, 'what's the big deal? You're
the only virgin I know.' "

I suggested to Lauren that we act out a dialogue, using
broken record and fogging.

INSISTENT DATE: Come on Lauren. Everybody's doing it.

LAUREN: That's certainly true. Everybody's doing it.
                    But I'm going to wait until I'm married.

INSISTENT DATE: Lauren, you're an old prude.

LAUREN: I'm an old prude, all right. Probably be
                    one until I'm married.

INSISTENT DATE: Yeah, but sex is really terrific. I know you'd really like it.

LAUREN: That's what I've heard. Sex is just great. I can't wait to get married.

You need never feel pressured into doing something because "everybody's" doing it. One example is oral sex. Men's magazines are full of oral sex and many men seem to expect it. But if you don't like oral sex, there is no reason for you to be pressured into it. Being pressured can diminish all your sexual pleasure. If you want to feel better about oral sex, you can with the techniques in chapters 4 and 5. But the choice is yours, not somebody else's. Any time you try to measure up to a standard in sex, sex itself tends to become unsexual and competitive.

A sexually sophisticated "scene" (or rather one that may, like the sexual playgrounds of the swingers' clubs, seem new or experimental) does not make the people in it sexually confident. Often, it has the opposite effect.

Sexual confidence means confidence in your own values and your own preferences. You try things and experiment, not because you ought to or have to — but because you want to.

In other words, sexual confidence does not come from joining a new group or assuming a new set of attitudes or having sex with a lot of different people.

Sexual confidence comes from unlearning someone else's values and developing your own values. And from learning, sharing, and exploring with someone else.

EXERCISES

Thought Stopping

1. Ten times a day:
   - Bring on the unwanted thought that interferes with your sexual pleasure.
   - The split second it begins to enter your mind, wipe it out by shouting, pounding, stamping your feet, digging a fingernail into your palm, snapping a rubber band around your wrist, and so on.
   - Then replace it with a positive, pleasurable image from your list — an image that is unrelated to the unwanted thought.

2. If the thought returns, drive it out again and replace it. This may require several repetitions before the thought will stay out for a period of time. You may need to drive it out as many as ten times.

3. Whenever, throughout the day, the unwanted thought or image appears in your mind, wipe it out at the first split second by shouting, stamping your feet, digging a fingernail into your palm, snapping a rubber band around your wrist. Do not let that thought develop. Replace that thought with an unrelated positive, pleasurable thought.

4. After practicing shouting "STOP," try hearing yourself "shout" "STOP" inside your mind, so that you can practice thought stopping silently, so that you can use the technique during lovemaking.

Silent Ridicule

1. Design a scene in which the authority figure looks, acts, and/or talks absurdly.
2. Practice alone, evoking the scene three to five times a day.
3. Whenever thoughts of that person intrude on your love-making, bring on the scene.

4

Unlearning Sexual Guilt

*Love bade me welcome; yet my soul
drew back, guilty of dust and sin.*
GEORGE HERBERT, 1593–1633

Guilt is a struggle between you and yourself.

You could call guilt a sense of original sin. Or the feeling that you deserve to be punished. *The American Heritage Dictionary* defines *guilt* as: "remorseful awareness of having done wrong." However you define guilt, it is a big subject. You could fill a library with books on guilt written by theologians, philosophers, and therapists. And you could fill another library with novels, poems, and plays whose central theme is guilt. Of that shadowy continent called guilt, where we all wander from time to time, I'd like to explore just one corner: sexual guilt.

Some people imagine that sexual guilt is a dark, warm, humid place, with the screech of unseen jungle creatures, the scent of perfume and decay, a mixture of danger and desire. But I've seen a great deal of sexual guilt and I don't think it's at all mysterious or romantic. A more accurate image for sexual guilt might be that of an old, damp blanket.

Of all the depressing feelings that you drag into bed, sexual guilt is probably the most common. And once you start carrying sexual guilt around with you, it feels natural, as if it had always been a part of you.

But it hasn't always been there. You weren't born feeling sexually guilty. Even if you have felt sexual guilt for as long as you can remember, you don't have to live with it now. Unlearn sexual guilt, throw off that dank, sad blanket, and it's extraordinary how much the whole world improves.

Guilt keeps you from being earthy and primitive. You can't jump for joy and howl and writhe with pleasure if you feel guilty. Guilt puts a distance between you and now. You can't be here, now, if you're worried about your parents or somebody else's idea of what you ought to do or not do.

Freedom from guilt is simply the constant opportunity to be wholly and magnificently yourself.

Sexual guilt oppresses you. It makes you feel less of a person, self-deprecating and afraid to experiment with, say, a new intercourse position or a fantasy or to take the initiative for making a change. Sexual guilt makes you hide inside the shell of what you expect other people expect of you. Gay men sometimes even go so far as to marry women, just to keep up appearances.

Guilt has the further effect of making people feel guilty about what they want — you are reluctant to suggest a change of pace or position, or to say "more" or "less" or "harder" or "softer," or to share any of the more complicated and interesting thoughts that you might have, if you feel sexually guilty.

Sexual guilt feeds on your pleasures and turns them sour. Specifically, sexual guilt is an anxiety that can cause strong men to lose their erections and passionate women to lose their desire. Guilt steals intimacy from lovemaking and makes sex mechanical, repetitious, and impersonal.

Some moralists might argue that sexual guilt has its uses, because it helps to deter sex crimes. I doubt that that is very often true. My clinical experience is that sexual offenders such

as exhibitionists, peeping Toms, and the anonymous feelers in
subway crowds are exaggerations of people ridden with sexual
guilt — impersonal, insensitive, frightened, and insatiable.
They are so crippled by guilt they are unable to function sexually in private, and so they go public. Guilt does not prevent
their crimes, it urges them on.

As a therapist, I see many people who feel sexually guilty.
They aren't criminals. They are touchingly innocent. What
makes them feel sexual guilt is the whole range of human sexual experience. Sexual pleasure. Touching themselves. Touching someone of the opposite sex. Touching someone of the
same sex. Oral sex. Fantasies about a neighbor or a talk-show
host. Tentative, awkward excursions outside the marriage bed.
Making love with the lights on. A sense of duty about what
they ought to enjoy sexually. Fear and confusion about what
they do enjoy.

Here's a partial list of the thoughts that commonly lead
people to feel sexual guilt:

— What I'm doing is wrong or shameful. Sex is only for mar-
   riage.
— Something bad will happen to me if I masturbate, or try
   oral sex, or have extramarital sex.
— There is something sinful about pleasure.
— "Nice girls" don't do this.
— I shouldn't be spending my time this way. There are other
   things I should be doing.
— I shouldn't enjoy this so much.
— If my parents knew I was doing this they would: (a) be
   ashamed of me, (b) hate me, (c) be disappointed in me,
   (d) punish me.

You can't feel sexy if you feel guilty. The guilt you feel is
directly proportional to the pleasure you don't feel.

LEARNING TO FEEL GUILTY

Children are sexual innocents. They touch their genitals with no sense of shame or embarrassment, but with discovery, wonder, and pleasure. Gradually or suddenly, slowly or in some grand humiliation, we all learn guilt. You can learn sexual guilt from parents, teachers, clergy, a bad experience, or from simply having wrong or incomplete information about sex.

A nine-year-old boy happily bouncing his erection underneath his short pants is threatened with expulsion from Cub Scouts by the den mother: "Most disgusting thing I've ever seen. Do that again and I'll send you home to your parents with a note."

An architectural student told me a particularly poignant story:

ANNE, TWENTY-TWO. "When I was eleven I discovered masturbating. Actually, I thought I'd invented it. I felt like Edison or Columbus. I'd discovered a whole new world, just as good as electricity or America. I called it "humamumming" like a hummingbird, and wrote down in a little book exactly how to do it so in case I died the rest of the people in the world would know how to do my discovery and be happy. My mother found the book and tore it up. She wouldn't tell me why."

We all begin as innocents and adventurers until guilt makes us afraid of our own pleasures.

EMMA, TWENTY-SEVEN, MOTHER OF TWO. "I have to confess I never felt that sex was all that terrific, but I fooled around a lot in high school, and I lived with Tom a year before we were married. My mother told me that sex was dirty before marriage and a duty after marriage. Mostly, to me, sex was something I just wanted to get through with as little hassle as possible, because I felt so guilty about doing something dirty.

I could never imagine my parents having sex. Maybe they had sex through a napkin. And while I guess I thought I was rebelling against their puritan righteousness when I had sex, I always had them in the back of my mind.

"My high school had a sex-education course. It taught us that sex was only for making children. When I think of the number of times in your life when sex is for making children compared to the number of times when it's because you love someone, or you're horny, it seems amazingly unbalanced. And then, too, they were big on disease. They had color close-up slides of what happens to genitals when you get a sexual disease. Like if you have sex, you're going to have a baby or running sores. But the most misleading part was what they left out. They left out almost everything. They left out warmth and affection, hugging and kissing, and most especially they left out pleasure. They never once mentioned pleasure.

"You know, if I'd known that sex wasn't 'dirty,' that sex could be loving and lovely, if I'd known about all the caressing and exploring and sharing, I wouldn't have wasted all that time just screwing."

"Just screwing" is a sad epidemic in our culture. So much hope and so much disappointment. Sex without passion, humor, or tenderness. Sex without love. Guilt and shame in our parents and teachers lead them to teach sex as if it were only for procreation. It's almost as if parents, teachers, and pornographers are in league to make us believe that sex is just genital friction, "just screwing." "Just screwing" is possibly the best reason there is for unlearning guilt.

Even the most loving and generous parents can, without meaning to, give their children the feeling that sex is shameful.

All parents are different. Some, like Emma's mother, tell us that sex is dirty or a duty. One woman says her mother answered her questions about sex by saying "It happens while you're sleeping." Telling their children about sex is a problem for most parents. They don't want to condone adolescent sex, so they keep quiet about the whole subject, as if knowledge made one promiscuous. (Sex research shows that most adolescents will engage in sex despite prohibitions from their parents, teachers, and religious advisers. The trouble is that without guidance and knowledge, sex in adolescence may be guilt-ridden and unpleasurable and may lead to tragic pregnancies.) Our parents' attitudes toward sex came from their own parents, whose attitudes came in turn from their parents. We have inherited Victorian taboos, religious misinformation, centuries of ignorance, and a certain amount of fear of a world that seems to encourage sex among strangers.

Our parents are only human, after all. But even with the best intentions they can cause a great deal of harm. Many of them don't say that sex is dirty but they are silent about sex. In their silence they give us guilt by default. As we grow up, these parents don't teach us that they are sexual. They don't even hint that they might enjoy lovemaking. So the most important models of our lives have missing pieces. Or so it seems. Many children grow up thinking that if their parents had two kids, they "did it" twice. Chances are that, in your own home, war, famine, politics, football, romance, school, cars, TV, and almost any other subject were open for discussion except one — sex. And when you begin to notice that your parents are never passionate, never take their clothes off in front of you, and give certain parts of your body evasive, cutesy nicknames, you begin to suspect that there is something secretive and shameful about passion, nudity, and sex organs. As you begin to have sexual feelings of your own in a home where the subject is never discussed except in the tersest, most evasive way, you know you have something to hide. "Playing with your wee-wee? Oh shame, shame, shame." Doing taboo things to your taboo body? Shame and silence upon you. You are guilty of an obscene crime.

Just imagine getting caught. You are lying on your bed in

your room, quietly, secretly masturbating, and your mother walks in. It is probably the worst crime of your life. It's bad enough to do it, but to get caught!

Masturbation is fundamental to who you are sexually. It is probably your first, and for many years your only, sexual experience. I believe that the guilt that most men feel about masturbation is the direct cause of the most common male sexual difficulty in bed, premature ejaculation. If most young men masturbate furtively and guiltily, they also masturbate in a hurry, because they are ashamed of what they are doing and the sooner it's over, the less chance there is of being caught. So a great many men grow up conditioned to ejaculate very quickly. Every man whom I have treated for premature ejaculation had a history of hurried, guilt-ridden masturbation. The opposite is also true. Men who were or are slow, relaxed, truly self-indulgent in their masturbation take much longer than other men to reach orgasm with their partner. As a result, I teach premature ejaculators ways to slow down and prolong their masturbation.

Similarly, most women who have never had an orgasm have never masturbated, because of guilt or lack of information. In fact, masturbation is the way many women who have never had an orgasm can learn to experience an orgasm.

But oh, the guilt and the shame that surrounds masturbation. No wonder so many people grow up feeling guilty about sex. Years ago a pediatrician told a young boy to "subdue" his urge to masturbate. When the child grew up and was an executive at a major corporation, he told his analyst that he felt guilty about masturbation. "Hmmm, you feel guilty about masturbation" was the analyst's only response. Assuming his guilt was justified, the executive suffered intense guilt for ten more years. Well, just what is it that is shameful about masturbation? Recently, in *How to Fall Out of Love,* I made a list of ten good things about masturbation.

1. It's pleasurable. It feels good. It's normal to masturbate.

Over thirty years ago, in 1948, a Kinsey survey showed that most people do masturbate (ninety-three per cent of men, sixty-seven per cent of women). It is now known and agreed in the scientific community that masturbation is normative. Most people do it.

2. It's not illegal, fattening, or life-shortening. And it's free. (And you can't say that about too many of life's other pleasures.)

3. Masturbation teaches you about your body and your own sexual responses. You tend to do what gives you the most pleasure. Knowing what those pleasures are makes it easier to teach someone else how to give you pleasure.

4. I have never known a couple who had the same sexual drives or needs. So often one wants to and the other doesn't. At those times, masturbation can be a caring and considerate compromise. It is also useful and practical when partners are separated or one partner is tired, or when the woman is in the last month of pregnancy.

5. To keep your sexual capabilities into your nineties, you need to stay sexually active. Masturbation doesn't use up sexual energy any more than running uses up the leg muscles. There will be times in your life when you will need masturbation to stay sexually active.

6. Self-reliance. Masturbation means that you can enjoy yourself, yourself. You don't have to rely on someone else for sexual pleasure. In fact, the strongest orgasm, physiologically speaking, is apt to be the one you have with yourself. The reason orgasm in masturbation is so often so intense is probably the instant feedback: you don't have to ask somebody to do this or that faster, slower, softer, or harder.

7. If you are comfortable with your own "self-loving," you are more likely to be comfortable with your children's natural exploratory needs and pleasures.

8. Masturbation is nonexploitative. You can enjoy sexual pleasures without making demands on someone else.

9. Masturbation is a good release of sexual tension. It's relaxing, it allows you to give a free range to your sexual fantasies, and, as a character in the play *The Boys in the Band* points out, you don't have to look your best.

10. And finally, masturbation can be a useful therapeutic technique. It's the most efficient way for women to learn to have an orgasm and for men to learn to delay ejaculation.

The list of bad things about masturbation can be summed up in a word: Nothing. Except the attitude that masturbation is shameful.

Masturbation is a pleasure. And human beings are especially endowed with a great capacity for pleasure. The woman's clitoris, for example, has nothing to do with procreation. The only function a clitoris has is to give pleasure. Isn't it remarkable that we humans have been given an organ that is only for sexual pleasure?

DIVINE SEX

The word *God* may seem oddly out of place in a book about sexuality. God and sex might seem to be, if not opposites, at least far removed from each other. Many young men and women have had to "confess" their "sins" of masturbation to their parish priest, week after week. Since the Christian religion teaches us, in part, that we are born in sin, some would have you believe that the love of pleasure is antithetical to the love of God. Let's examine that assumption for a moment.

People tend to keep their religion unchanged (along with their sexual guilt), just as it was in their childhood. Or they throw out their religion altogether when they find that a childhood God doesn't work in an adult world. Whether or not you feel it is time to re-evaluate some aspects of your own religion, I think there are two very important points to be made. First, religion can be one of the major sources of sexual guilt.

And second, it can be one of the major sources for *relieving* sexual guilt.

For Christianity this paradox is easily explained. Much of what has become a tradition of sexual guilt stems from Saint Augustine, the fifth-century theologian who argued that because of original sin, sexual pleasure distracts from the pursuit of God. He said that sex was only for the purpose of creating life, and permissible only between husband and wife. On the other hand, Saint Thomas Aquinas, the thirteenth-century monk whose thinking is basic to much of Catholic doctrine, said that your conscience takes precedence over church doctrine. (Saint Thomas was quite clear about what a conscience is. It is not a still, small voice. Conscience is an intellectual discipline — a thoughtful judgment based on an informed assessment as to the good or evil of an act. Conscience is hard-headed reason making a judgment that adds to the purpose of your life.) This thought, that your conscience is your ultimate guide, leads many modern theologians to take issue with the strict notion that intercourse is permissible only for procreation.

One Catholic theologian puts it this way: "The question is not whether it's in or out of marriage, hetero- or homosexual, for creation or for pleasure, but is there warmth and beauty between two human beings? Are they hurting anyone? Is there love?"

The Reverend Dr. William Kirby, a Protestant theologian, states, "Let's start with love. Is sex loving? Sex before or after marriage or between two individuals of the same or different sex cannot simply be placed into a category of good or bad or wrong or right or liberating or confining, but rather whether it is loving. The situation is as individual as you are. You will make your own decisions based on your own values . . . the value you place on intimacy, on marriage, on other people, and on yourself."

Another Catholic theologian adds, "Sexual pleasure is a gift

of God. And as such it doesn't need to have some other purpose if it draws a person outside merely selfish concerns and
into involvement with another person."

Judaism seems to have much less of a tradition of sexual
guilt. Theologian and author Rabbi Reeve Brenner points out:
"To Jews, sex is a blessing. For thousands of years Jews have
been instructed to read the Song of Songs before going to bed
on the Sabbath. It is a very erotic poem. You see, Jewish tradition encourages the love act. The Sabbath is supposed to be
devoted to rest, reinvigoration of body and soul, and it is a day
for love. In the Hebrew Bible (the Old Testament) and in the
Talmud, Judaism makes a strong argument *against* celibacy
and *for* the raptures of love. And the rabbis of the Talmud
encouraged the many varieties of the love act. For the Jew,
sin is failure to make full use of the gifts God has given us. One
of the most prominent and obvious gifts of all is sex."

The theologians I have cited here would agree, despite their
different religious backgrounds, that the Word of God, as seen
in the Bible and the Talmud, celebrates sexuality and invites
you to join in the celebration. The conditions of joining are
open to interpretation, but the invitation is clear. Religion, say
these theologians, should relieve sexual guilt, not cause it.

I would like to add my own point of view. Every time I go
to the Sloan-Kettering Institute for Cancer Research in New
York City, and I see people who are dying, some of them quite
young, I am struck with the amazing value of life, and the fact
that it is a temporary gift. Seeing death so nearby gives me a
profound sense of renewal. All of us will face death. Perhaps
tomorrow. But in the meantime we have this moment and this
day to live — to experience joy and pleasure. And if you are
not exploiting or hurting someone, why deny yourself sexual
pleasure? For sexual pleasure is a magnificent affirmation of
life.

I also believe, on the other hand, that as soon as you are
sexually involved with another person you are also involved
with significant responsibility. Let me explain. Impersonal,

nonintimate, exploitative sex means that someone is being hurt. Sex can be the most intimate interchange with another person. But if one person is being exploitative and the other person thinks that he or she is being intimate, there can be serious casualties — even tragedies.

So I am not arguing for the total elimination of guilt. If guilt can inhibit people from taking advantage of someone who is lonely or idolizes them or is dependent on them or is just sexually convenient, then guilt has a positive role to play. But guilt alone is not enough. If someone takes advantage of someone else and feels guilty about it, but doesn't change and continues to take advantage of people, nothing worthwhile has happened. When guilt leads to someone's giving instead of just taking, a person's making constructive changes, then guilt has a place.

Sex can also lead to pregnancy. Therefore, you and your partner should understand and share responsibility for contraception.

The real point here is that sexual pleasure involves responsibility, a contraceptive responsibility and an emotional responsibility. It's a responsibility you cannot really avoid, even if you both decide to spend, say, just one afternoon or evening together in bed.

UNLEARNING GUILT

A young Hamlet lies on his analyst's couch, his arm flung over his eyes: "Oh where, where does this guilt come from? From my dead father or oh, my holy mother? Why this guilt that makes fungus of my passion, open sores of my love. Oh why, oh why am I guilty?"

Let us shut the door, quietly.

Guilt is an emotion you learn. Since you have learned to feel sexual guilt, you can also unlearn it.

Not only can you unlearn sexual guilt, you can unlearn it

without changing values you don't want to change. You don't have to be someone else, or join some group or sect, or become promiscuous or "chaste" to lose your feelings of sexual guilt. The whole point of unlearning sexual guilt is to keep the values you value but to keep them out of a fresh sense of their importance, rather than out of guilt. Unlearning guilt means throwing off other people's programming of your sexuality so you are free to be creative and confident in your feelings; free to choose according to your values and free to experience your own pleasure and beauty.

The first technique for unlearning guilt, "graduated calming," is at the heart of behavior therapy. Used primarily to dispel anxieties and fears, graduated calming (or "desensitization") was developed by Dr. Joseph Wolpe, the father of behavior therapy. Dr. Wolpe observed, in a series of clinical studies, that negative feelings such as guilt tend to cancel out positive emotions such as love or pleasure or feeling happy. The reverse, he noted, is also true. You don't feel guilty if you feel deeply relaxed or highly sexual. You don't feel great anger when you are feeling great love. There are mixtures, certainly. You can and do feel both love and anger or guilt and pleasure or even all four emotions at once. However, the essential principle — that positive emotions tend to block negative emotions — has great therapeutic value when used systematically. Let me describe how graduated calming works.

Graduated calming is relearning on a neurological and emotional level. It takes you slowly, step by step, up a ladder (or "hierarchy," as behavior therapists call it) of the things that make you feel anxious. As you calm your smaller anxieties, your larger feelings of anxiety become less intense. Here's how it works. You begin with a positive emotional state — relaxation or erotic arousal — then imagine a scene or engage in an activity that usually causes you to feel a little anxiety, and then return to the positive state (relaxation or erotic arousal). Graduated calming is very much like the way a mother (or father) might teach her (his) young child not to be afraid of the sea. The first day, while holding the child close to her, which is reassuring and calming to the child, the mother shows the child the sea from the top of a dune. The next day she walks closer to the sea from the top of a dune. The next day she walks closer to the sea while holding the child. The next day they go closer. And so on, closer and closer (graduated approach), constantly reassuring her child (repetition is a low-anxiety environment), until the child becomes familiar with the strange new environment and feels relaxed enough to get his feet wet.

Similarly, for sexual guilt you gradually, step by step, approach whatever it is that makes you feel guilt. You keep on getting closer, never close enough to feel guilty and always relaxed enough or sexually excited enough to feel calm or pleasure. With repetition and a graduated, systematic approach, a new learning takes place. You learn to face without guilt what used to inspire guilt. And you unlearn the guilt you used to feel.

There are two ways to do graduated calming. The easier makes use of a real-life, controlled situation like the one the mother used with her child at the seashore. We will call it direct calming (*in vivo* desensitization), and I will teach it to you next. The second technique, called simply graduated calming, is more complex, and I will save it for the next chapter. However, it can be very helpful for dealing with guilt, and you may want to read about it before deciding how to deal with your particular guilt problem.

Direct Calming

Sexual guilt takes chameleon forms. You may not feel guilty as such, you may feel headachy or experience a sudden drop in sexual excitement. Sexual guilt can disguise itself as feelings of disgust, sweaty palms, or feeling uneasy. One woman described her guilty feelings as her "Granny's knot" in her stomach, referring to her stern, humorless grandmother.

LAURIE, THIRTY-EIGHT-YEAR-OLD MAGAZINE EDITOR. When she was a child, Laurie's home was always spotlessly clean. One of her first experiences with sex was playing "doctor" with a boy next door. They were both eleven and they were very curious. "Oh, that's what that looks like. What does this do?" Her grandmother caught them, spanked the little boy and sent him home, spanked Laurie and told her "Never ever let a man touch you before you are married. Now wash your hands." As Laurie grew older, her mother (who was just as stern as her grandmother) also gave her the feeling that sex was dirty and nasty. When Laurie, having only the vaguest idea of what sex was, asked her mother what oral sex was, her mother told her it was "something whores do to men." Laurie had to ask the other kids what a whore was.

After twelve years of marriage, Laurie was concerned about the "staleness" of making love with her husband. "I'd like to do more with Jake. He wants me to do oral sex with him. And I'd like to, but . . . I tried twice and ended up crying. I felt so stupid and clumsy. And terribly guilty. I kept imagining my mother thinking I was a whore."

Part of Laurie's problem was in simply not knowing how. I explained several techniques to her and suggested that her husband could let her know when it felt good, not so good, and sensational. "There isn't any one 'right' way," I told her, "just the ways he likes it best." But Laurie still had a strong dislike for the "messiness" of oral sex. And it still made her feel very guilty.

So I told Laurie that we were going to use erotic feelings as a counterconditioner for guilt. "We're going to let pleasure inhibit guilt," I said, "instead of the other way around."

I asked Laurie to make up a list (hierarchy) on a scale of zero to one hundred of the specific things about oral sex that made her feel guilty when she and Jake made love. Zero, I told her, would be absolutely relaxed and one hundred would be total panic.

Here are what guilt levels mean in terms of what you feel:

GUILT SCALE

0   Total relaxation. No guilt.

10–20   Mild guilt, not very noticeable.

30–50   Moderate guilt. Definitely feeling uneasy. Beginnings of a tension headache. "Butterfly" feelings in your stomach. Some muscle tension.

60–70   High level of guilt. Heart pounding. Head- or stomachache. Real distress and discomfort.

80–90   Intense, severe guilt, approaching panic. Something you want to avoid at all costs.

100   Panic. Emotional chaos. The most guilt you can possibly imagine.

And here is the hierarchy Laurie drew up to describe the guilt she felt when she was making love with Jake.

LAURIE'S LIST

10   Messiness. Getting "slippery stuff" (her own lubrication or Jake's ejaculate) on her hands.

20   Getting "slippery stuff" on her thighs.

30   Getting "slippery stuff" on her stomach.

40   Giving Jake's penis a light kiss.

50   Taking the head of his penis in her mouth.

60   Running her tongue around the tip of his penis.

70   Running her tongue up and down the shaft of his penis.

80   Kissing Jake's testicles.

90   Getting ejaculate in her mouth.

95   Taking his whole penis (as much as possible) in her mouth and moving it in and out of her mouth.

100   Her mother knowing she was doing this.

The list terrified her. We began in the office with hand cream to simulate ejaculate fluid. "Here, Laurie, put a little lotion on your hands. Feel how slippery it is." When she could do that without feeling guilty or anxious she was able to enjoy the sensual, tactile feeling of slippery lotion between her fingers. "Sex isn't always neat and tidy. It can be slippery and messy. It's full of sights and sounds your mother would never allow in her kitchen," I told her.

Laurie did the rest of her hierarchy at home. She read erotic passages from her favorite novels until she felt aroused, then put a little of her own lubricant first on her thighs and then when she was comfortable with that, on her stomach.

"The next time you go to bed with Jake take a nice warm bath first and read some erotic passages from a book that you find arousing — a Harold Robbins book or perhaps *The Pearl*. Turn the lights low and turn on some music. Begin to make out with Jake. The point is to feel warm and comfortable, relaxed, and very sexual. You need a lot of sexual pleasure to block a little guilt.

"Direct calming takes a certain amount of repetition, so you'll have to explain the technique to Jake beforehand. When you are feeling highly aroused, kiss Jake's penis briefly and stop if you feel the least bit guilty. Do a little erotic reading or some more making out.

"And then when you are feeling erotic and back at zero on your guilt scale, kiss his penis again, briefly. Continue doing this until you can kiss his penis and feel no guilt or discomfort. That may take a few minutes. It's more likely to take somewhat longer."

It took Laurie five weeks to work her way up her hierarchy, and unlearn her guilt about oral sex.

"Now it gives me pleasure to give him so much pleasure. I knew it was working when I stopped wondering if my mother would think I was a whore. That was when I started enjoying taking Jake's penis in my mouth."

Here is the direct-calming procedure that you can follow to reduce guilt. When you are feeling you are at zero, relaxed and sexually aroused with no guilt feelings, do the lowest thing on your guilt scale. The instant you feel the slightest discomfort or guilt, stop, go back to doing something that will cause you to feel sensual and erotic so that your discomfort will be reduced, and wait until your discomfort is reduced to zero before you try your first step again. When you can do that first step without feeling any discomfort or guilt, move on to the next step in your hierarchy.

Before you draw up your own guilt hierarchy, let's look at a few more examples.

Chris and Patricia were very much in love. Both graduate students at a large Southern university, they did not want to marry before they finished school. Patricia's mother's opposition to sex before marriage and the prohibitions of Patricia's church about premarital sex made powerful impressions on her. Yet she had decided that she wanted to be Chris's lover. "But I would like to love Chris without these awful feelings of guilt and remorse." Together we drew up a guilt hierarchy. You've no doubt noted how often I've said "Go slowly, one step at a time." Chris and Patricia took eighteen months to work through her hierarchy. They would spend a month or two learning about necking and kissing until Patricia felt comfortable with her erotic feelings. Then they would move the next step up the scale, cautiously, tentatively, until she felt no guilt about, say, petting. When they made love for the first time, it was full of love and pleasure. And free of guilt, something that would not have been possible had they made love before going through Patricia's hierarchy for eighteen months, "slowly, one step at a time."

PATRICIA'S GUILT HIERARCHY

0   Relaxed. Reading or listening to music together.

10   Hugging, touching, and kissing with their clothes on.

20   Patricia lying on top of Chris, fully clothed.

30   Petting, Chris touching Patricia's genitals through her clothes.

40   Sleeping together, Patricia wearing a nightgown.

50   Patricia caresses Chris's genitals through his clothes.

60   Patricia caresses his genitals. They are both nude.

70   Sleeping together in the nude.

80   Oral sex.

90   Intercourse.

So many things can make people feel guilty. People feel guilty about their fantasies ("I must be really sick to imagine making love to Donald Duck and Mickey Mouse"). Some feel guilty about just wanting sex ("Why can't I walk down the street without lusting for one woman after another?"). Some feel guilty about being homosexual, some about receiving pleasure. Pleasure itself, in strong conflict with our old puritan ethic, makes some people feel ashamed of themselves. Masturbating makes millions feel needlessly guilty. And oral sex and kissing a breast and holding a penis — all the things that loving human beings do to give each other and themselves pleasure — make some people feel guilty.

If you want to stop feeling sexually guilty, make a list of the things that make you feel sexual guilt. Take just one item on your list, break it down into component parts, and draw up a hierarchy. Later you can take another item and do the same with it. Here's a masturbation hierarchy, for example.

MASTURBATION HIERARCHY

0   Lying down with no clothes on, listening to music.

10   Lying down with no clothes on, knowing I'm going to masturbate.

25 Touching myself on the thighs.

40 Touching my nipples.

60 Holding my penis / touching my clitoris.

75 Rubbing my penis / clitoris.

85 Having an orgasm masturbating.

Once you have your hierarchy, the next step is to feel erotic. Use fantasies, making out, soft lights, soft music, sexy pictures, sexy books to help you reach a fairly high level of arousal. Although erotic feelings can block guilt feelings, you need, as I've mentioned, a lot of arousal to stop a little guilt.

But a little guilt is all you need to defeat.

An interesting point about a direct-calming hierarchy is that as you move the bottom item down from, say, fifteen to zero, you also move all the other items down the scale in guilt. So after you conquer the item labeled ten on your guilt hierarchy, your second item, the one you perhaps labeled twenty, becomes ten.

When you are feeling sexually aroused, do the first item on your list for a few moments, or until you feel the first pangs of guilt. Then stop. For example, if the first item on your list is having your breast touched ("breasts are for feeding a baby, not for pleasure"), have your partner just lightly touch your breasts, then stop as soon as you feel any guilt.

The point is to repeat each step until you don't feel guilty doing it, always stopping the instant you feel the least hint of guilt. And do not repeat the activity until you are at zero again, and feeling erotic. Erotic feelings compete with guilt.

Always be careful to move up only ten or, at the most, twenty points on the scale to the next scene. You want to be sure that pleasure always wins and that guilt always loses, so that pleasure is learned and guilt is unlearned.

Direct calming is the most powerful and comprehensive technique to use in dispelling guilt. But it is not the only technique. Here are a few more therapeutic exercises for guilt.

They are relatively easy to do and, used to supplement direct or graduated calming — or, in some cases of low-level guilt, used all on their own — they can be very effective.

Thought Stopping

The instant an old, familiar guilty thought comes creeping into your mind ("It's a sin to touch yourself there, my son." "Nice girls never open their legs in front of a gentleman." "Priscilla, Lord rest her soul, wouldn't want me to do this." "It's not normal for a man to want a man." "Pleasure is a waste of time." "Mother would kill me if she knew." "Unfaithful, unfaithful, unfaithful"), shut it out, cut it off, stop it by silently shouting "STOP" to yourself, and replace that thought with a pleasurable thought. If you are engaging in a sexual activity, replace the guilt-producing thought by filling your mind with the physical sensations you are feeling at the moment: the finely pebbled roughness of a tongue on a slippery clitoris, the slow, tingling trace of a fingernail down the inside of a thigh.

Assertive Dialogues

Finally, assertive dialogues ("conversations in the back of your head" from chapter 3) is an effective technique, particularly for dealing with religious guilt. If, for example, you feel guilty about using contraception (because your church forbids it) and you'd like to overcome that guilt, you might hold imaginary conversations in the back of your mind that sound something like this:

PRIEST: Shame. You're using a contraceptive.

YOU: Yes, that's right, I'm using a contraceptive.

PRIEST: You know the Pope has said that's a serious sin.

YOU: Yes, but I've thought this out as thoroughly as I can.
          And I'm going to keep on using a contraceptive.

PRIEST: But just recently the Pope said —

YOU: Sure. I know what the Pope says. But Saint Thomas
          said that conscience takes precedence over church
          doctrine, even the Pope's. And my conscience tells
          me that contraception is a moral necessity.

PRIEST: It's a terrible sin, my child.

YOU: Yes, a sin. I must follow my conscience. Saint
          Thomas says following your conscience is no sin.

Here's how you, a homosexual, might imagine a conversation between yourself and a minister:

MINISTER: Homosexuality is a sin because it's unnatural.

YOU: It's natural to me. For me, it's making love.

MINISTER: The Bible says it's against the law of God for a
          man to lie with another man.

YOU: The Bible may say it's against God's law. But it
          is love. And the law of love is God's law.

It might seem to some that these three techniques — direct
calming, thought stopping, and assertive dialogues — are too
simple to take on the whole rolling momentum of generations
of guilt. Indeed, they are simple and easy to do. That is their
beauty. You don't have to spend half your lifetime to decrease
your sexual guilt and increase your pleasure.

The Victorians believed that cures had to taste terrible and
be taken in quantity over time to be effective. But we know
better now. Drugs work better against tuberculosis than do
years in a mountain sanatorium. You don't need to wait for
years to be free from anxiety and guilt. Not when you can be
free from them now.

EXERCISES

Direct Calming

1. Through masturbation, or reading erotic scenes, or your partner's caresses, reach a high level of erotic arousal.

2. Tentatively try the lowest item on your guilt hierarchy.

3. If you feel *any* guilt or anxiety, stop doing that activity.

4. Relax and go back to feeling erotic pleasure until you feel no guilt or anxiety.

5. Try the activity again and continue doing it. But, again, if you feel any guilt or anxiety, stop doing it.

6. Go back to reading or touching until you get to zero guilt or anxiety.

7. When you can do the activity for about twenty seconds and still feel yourself so relaxed that your guilt and anxiety are zero, savor how relaxed you feel with this activity.

8. Continue the whole process (at a later time, if you wish) with the next item on your hierarchy.

5

Unlearning Sexual Anxiety

If you can make it through this chapter, the rest is easy.

The old-time amusement parks used to have a ride called something like "Crypt of the Vampires" or "Grotto of the Zombies," "Tunnel of Horrors" or "The Morgue." All the amusement parks had one. It was the scary ride. You and your date climbed into a little car or boat and went riding off into the dark. You could hear screams in the distance. Then, as you were nervously edging closer to each other on the seat, flashing lights and buzzers went off, and a giant vampire came down from the ceiling. A little farther down, a headless axman held his head by the hair. Skeletons rattled and corpses sat up in their coffins. It was a popular ride with young couples, because it was a perfect excuse to leap into each other's arms. You could even steal a kiss and feel around a little in the dark interval between the moaning man with a knife in his chest and the giant gorilla. In fact, it was great for necking in the days when necking was a secret, stolen pleasure. All that mechanical trickery wasn't really that scary. You knew you would emerge at the end of the ride into the afternoon sun or the warm summer evening.

In reality, some people never do emerge from their tunnels of Sexual Anxiety. What they see and hear, of course, aren't zombies or vampires. It's more apt to be a father's voice re-

minding you that your body's too fat or too thin, or that that's
a dirty thing to do. It's more apt to be mocking eyes peering at
your penis — "too small, too small" — quiet voices discussing
your technique or criticizing your feelings, faceless mouths
with secret words guaranteed to make you squirm.

Oh, the vague and squirmy churnings of sexual anxiety —
muscles twitch and knot, hearts pound, and stomachs turn
queasy. In sex, anxiety is a barrier that prevents you from feeling pleasure. Often when you have anxiety during sex, you
just feel numb.

What I would like to do is lift the lid on those nightmarish
crawly creatures, those sexual anxieties that haunt us in our
beds at night, and see what they look like in the light of day,
see where they come from, what their names are, whom they
persecute, and what makes them go away.

You've already dealt with one of the toughest sexual anxieties, sexual guilt. Now it's time to finish house cleaning and
deal with any other sexual anxiety you may still feel.

Sexually related anxiety occurs in almost everyone. There
seems to be no common denominator. Sexual anxiety crosses
cultures, classes, professions, and geography. Doctors, lawyers,
housewives, high-powered executives are as afflicted by it as
truck drivers and astronauts. Psychiatrists have their share.
Homosexuals, bisexuals, heterosexuals, young students, surf-
ers, and learned professors all appear to be susceptible to anxiety when they engage in sex.

Many assume that high-school and college students and
young singles are immune to the afflictions of sexual anxiety,
that they operate on another sexual frontier. It's part of our
cultural mythology that the children of the age of sexual liberation can come and go sexually as they please, floating on a
high of sensual pleasure. It's a beguiling myth, but most young
single adults are having a hard time on the frontiers of sexual
freedom. They are trying to do things they were raised *not* to
do. And they suffer anxiously for it. A phrase from another

generation, "too much, too soon," could be a banner for this new generation.

Like sexual guilt, the other sexual anxieties lead to sex without sensation, silent, mechanistic sex. Sex without intimacy or caring.

LEARNING ANXIETIES

Cultural stereotypes haunt us all. Men have the sexual athlete, the "get it up anywhere, any time" macho man, in their hall of anxieties. The macho image denies what is beautiful in men — their capacity for understanding, for love, for dignity, warmth, and affection. And it denies their exquisite sensitivity to pleasure, as if all erotic pleasure were in the penis and the rest of the body were numb. Not the least of the cruelties of this stereotype is the anxiety it generates, as men try to live up to its super-sex image, no matter what the circumstances.

Stereotypes for women have changed. Once upon a time, women were not supposed to be sexual. They weren't supposed to find pleasure in sex, let alone indulge in pleasure. And they weren't supposed to be assertive, to take the initiative. They were supposed to stay home, lie still, and bear children. As oppressive as that old role was, I'm not at all sure the new role causes any less anxiety.

Now there are new achievement stereotypes for women. "Go out and run a corporation." "Be a brain surgeon." I think most women are delighted that these and other career opportunities are opening up to women. But the demands of performance and success create just as much anxiety for women as for men. And now there is a new female sexual burden. Some women feel inadequate if they don't have multiple orgasms. Women, say the slick magazines, should be expert, accomplished lovers, who can turn a man on or off with the flick of a wrist, should practice intricate oral sex, and so on.

Otherwise, so the stereotype goes, they are inadequate and incomplete.

It's a shame so many people believe in the sexual stereotypes created by the mass media. But it's understandable. Stereotypes are everywhere, while there just aren't very many realistic models. You rarely, if ever, see other real people making real love — being awkward, playful, and loving. And what child can imagine his or her parents having a terrific time making love together, groaning, moaning, writhing, and being passionate? The conflict between the reality of making love and trying to live up to the imagined perfection of stereotypes is one common cause of anxiety.

Parents, keeping their secrets, unwittingly pass along their anxieties with their guilt. Centerfold magazines celebrate genitalia and breasts. Sexual-advice columns tell you ten new ways to achieve sexual prowess every month. In media mythology women are nubile, airbrushed, and willing; the men tall, handsome, and successful, untroubled by the hassles of everyday life. The school of anxiety has many teachers. Let me mention a few more besides parents and cultural stereotypes.

Any bad sexual experience tends to linger long after it's over. I've mentioned the first slap of the baby's hand away from his/her genitals that had lifelong reverberations of guilt and anxiety. Rape or being molested understandably often causes long-term anxiety. Having sex because you feel you have to — because it's a marital duty or a honeymoon ritual, or proof of your sexuality, or because everyone else does — can haunt you with anxiety.

Then there are the misconceptions, the belief that something is necessary, or important, or bad, or weird when it just isn't so. One woman dreaded spending another night with her lover because she felt she was inadequate for not having "vaginal orgasms."

I explained to her that there is no such thing as a "vaginal" orgasm, any more than there is a breast or a foot orgasm (see chapter 2). An orgasm is an all-over body response to pleasure. How and where you receive that pleasure is a matter of what works for you, not of "right and wrong." Once she understood that it was fine to have an orgasm with her lover's hands, she felt infinitely better.

Some men feel anxious because they think their penis should be harder or longer. Nonsense, of course, but anxiety isn't based on good sense. Yet when anxiety is based simply on misconceptions, a fact may be enough to dispel the anxiety. Sometimes all a man needs to know are the general facts about penis length (when they're erect there is rarely much variation in length) and hardness (rocklike is not necessarily the most sensual texture) to appreciate that his male sexuality isn't measured by his penis.

Unfortunately, however, most anxiety goes beyond simple misconceptions, and facts aren't enough "medicine." Most anxiety is emotionally learned. Unlearning most anxiety, therefore, is an emotional exercise.

Listed below are some of the more common sexual anxieties. Skim quickly through them and see if some of them sound familiar. (This is not a complete list. No list could be complete.)

Common (*and a Few Uncommon*) Anxieties

Losing Control: Fear of being vulnerable. Being afraid to let go, howl, shout, and writhe.

Being Looked At: Fear of looking silly or unattractive. "My body is ugly." "With my clothes off, I'll be a disappointment." "I'm too fat." "My scars will show."

Vagina Fears: Looking at. Being looked at. Being touched. Touching. Oral sex. Getting "caught" in the vagina.

Penis Fears: Looking at. Being looked at. Touching. Oral sex. Size. Smells. Secretions.

Having Sex When You Don't Want To: Out of duty, ceremony (just got married), "to keep him," peer pressure. "Everybody does it on the first date."

Performance Fears — General Inhibitions and Worries: "Am I doing it right?" "Will I last long enough?" "Am I going to have an orgasm?" "Will I have an erection?" "Will I lose the erection?" "Am I as good as his/her other lovers?" "What does he/she want me to do now?" "Will I lubricate?" "We've gone too far." "Are the kids asleep?"

What Do I Say?: ? ? ? ? ? ? ? ? ?

Oral Sex: "How do you do it?" "Do I have to do it?" Germs. Smells. Secretions. "This is an abnormal thing to do."

Penetration: "It will hurt." "I don't want to do it." "My mother [father, brother, sister, husband, wife, teacher, doctor, lover, roommate, priest, minister, rabbi, boss, best friend] will hate, loathe, despise, and be disappointed in me."

Acting Out a Fantasy: "I'll look silly." "This is sick, crazy."

Female Assertiveness / Male Assertiveness: Initiating sex play. Stating desire for sex.

Masturbation: Guilt. "Am I harming myself?" "Will I get caught?" "This is second-rate."

Breast Fears: Too big. Too small. Droopy. Being touched. Being kissed.

Passivity: "I'm not in control." "I'm being selfish. I shouldn't be taking pleasure, I should be giving more."

Joseph Wolpe defines anxiety as a person's "characteristic pattern of autonomic responses to noxious stimulation." Perhaps I should add that anxiety is a characteristic pattern of responses to what you perceive as noxious stimulation. If having your breast stroked makes you uneasy, worried, tense, and uncertain about what is going to happen next, then having your breast stroked is what Dr. Wolpe calls noxious stimulation. Of course anxiety can be perfectly realistic. Having your breast stroked by someone who holds a knife to your throat is anything but reassuring. But what we want to get rid of are the anxieties you feel when there is no real threat.

For in this complex, unruly, unpredictable world, it would be a great relief to know that there is one safe place — a bedroom, a kitchen, a meadow on the side of a mountain, wherever you next make love — that is free from anxiety.

Go over the list of anxieties above and pick out any that apply to you, that interfere with your sexual pleasure. Choose one that you would like to begin to conquer.

UNLEARNING ANXIETIES

Bans

When something causes anxiety my first advice is apt to be very simple and direct: "Stop doing it. Ban it."

Often bans are the first and only step to unlearning anxiety. This is particularly true for performance anxieties.

EUGENE, FORTY-EIGHT-YEAR-OLD CORPORATE EXECUTIVE. Eugene had been having erection problems for ten years. Sex was a trial for him, because he was increasingly worried about whether or not he would have an erection. "It would be bad enough," he said, "if I only worried about it when it didn't happen. But I worry about it during the day, when I should be concentrating on business. And late at night long after I should be asleep. The more I think about it the worse it gets. And if I ever do get an erection, I'm scared it will be my last one. As soon as I get scared, my erection goes away."

Eugene agreed that as part of his therapy he would ban intercourse.

It was as if I had prescribed a miracle erection drug. Eugene stopped worrying about whether or not he would get an erection because he couldn't use it if he did. When he stopped having anxiety about erections, he started having erections. He and his wife had a wonderful time, cuddling, kissing, touching, and playing. For the first time in years they really turned on to each other sexually. "It's like a Garden of Eden," he said, "there's so much pleasure." "You ought to do a book called *Ban Intercourse*. It's the best medicine there is," he said. Eventually, he broke the ban. But in the first weeks, while he kept to the ban, he learned more about sexuality and pleasure than he had in his previous forty-eight years.

When you worry about your lovemaking, when you scrutinize it and keep score, you interfere with the natural flow of sexual feelings. You might place a ban on erections or orgasms, if those things cause you anxiety. The point is to stop now, immediately, doing anything in sex that causes you anxiety. That allows sexual feelings to develop. It begins to change accounting or keeping score ("When was the last time I had an erection?" "Is it time for another one?" "How many orgasms have I had tonight so far? Two? Three?") into loving and caring.

Very often when someone is anxious about some aspect of sexual performance, such as having an erection or an orgasm, I'll suggest taking the ban one step further, into "paradoxical intention," a technique (developed by the psychiatrist Viktor Frankl) that helps you to do something by not doing it. I advise a man to ban not only intercourse but also his erection, to tell it to go away when it occurs or as it is about to occur. The paradox is that your body, freed of the anxiety of "will I, won't I?" may go its own merry way and have an orgasm or erection, as the case may be. I don't tell people the whole story. When they ask why I'm telling them to get rid of the one thing they are so anxious about having, I simply smile and say, "You'll see."

By the time you lift a ban, chances are you've learned a very important lesson. Relaxed, playful sex, making love without pressure to perform, and removing the goal of orgasm all intensify your arousal. Erections and excitement usually happen naturally, when you don't work on them. When the pressure to have an orgasm is off, your chances of orgasm increase,

because anxiety about your performance is no longer interfering with your pleasure.

Simply stopping doing the things that cause you anxiety isn't
always, by itself, enough to cure the anxiety. Especially if the
anxiety isn't about performance. But a ban is the first essential
step. If you continue to do something that causes intense anxiety, the anxiety may grow even stronger and spread. So stop
first. Later you can use direct or graduated calming to unlearn
your anxiety and begin to enjoy what used to make you feel
anxious.

*

Pleasure, both sexual and sensual, is one of the best antidotes
to sexual anxiety. Anxiety and erotic pleasure are at opposite ends of the balance scale. As anxiety rises, sexual pleasure falls. And as pleasure rises, anxiety falls. It's not a one-to-
one balance; you need a lot of pleasure to overcome a little
anxiety. That's at the heart of behavior therapy: not taking on
all of your sexual anxiety at once, but just a little, one step at
a time. So that pleasure always wins. And anxiety always loses.

Feel very good when you do a little of something that is
anxiety-producing, and you'll find you won't feel so anxious.
Feel very good repeatedly, in the presence of high erotic pleasure or deep relaxation, and you will unlearn anxiety as you
learn to experience pleasure.

In the last chapter you learned how to use direct calming to combat guilt. The same technique works against other
anxieties.

MARGARET, FORTY-TWO-YEAR-OLD FILM DIRECTOR. "It's not
that I don't like sex, it's just that I have a hard time getting
started. When Felix starts touching me I feel anxious and just
want to get away. What I hate is the feeling that I'm out of
control, not knowing what's going to happen next or when.
If only I were more in control of the situation I wouldn't feel

so left out. I'd really like to initiate and be seductive at least once in a while, but just thinking about that makes me feel anxious."

I gave Margaret a pencil and paper. "Let's make a list of the seductive things you could do that make you feel anxious. Then we'll list them in ascending order of anxiety. The list is called an anxiety hierarchy."

Zero is feeling totally relaxed and calm, with no anxiety, and a hundred is the highest anxiety imaginable. Here are what anxiety levels mean in terms of what you feel:

ANXIETY SCALE

0	Total relaxation. No anxiety.
10–20	Mild anxiety, not very noticeable.
30–50	Moderate anxiety. Definitely feeling uneasy. Beginnings of tension headache. "Butterfly" feelings in your stomach. Some muscle tension.
60–70	High level of anxiety. Heart pounding. Head- or stomachache. Real distress and discomfort.
80–90	Intense, severe anxiety, approaching panic. Something you want to avoid at all costs.
100	Panic. Emotional chaos. The most anxiety you can possibly imagine.

Here is Margaret's anxiety hierarchy for initiating sex:

MARGARET'S ANXIETY HIERARCHY

0	Relaxed, listening to classical music.
10	Putting her hand on Felix's shoulder.
20	Kissing him on the neck.
30	Running her hand inside his shirt.
40	Putting her hand in Felix's pocket.

50   Wearing a nightgown in front of Felix in the afternoon.

60   Taking Felix's hands to her breasts. Running her tongue inside his mouth.

70   Walking nude in front of Felix when he's not expecting it.

80   Saying to Felix: "I want to make love."

90   Unzipping his fly and reaching inside.

100   Waking Felix up from his Sunday-afternoon nap by stroking his penis.

Margaret enjoyed fantasizing, and reaching a high level of arousal was not difficult for her. She fantasized, and when she felt erotic she walked up to Felix and put her hand on his shoulder. He turned slightly to look at her and Margaret kissed him on the neck. "Then I went back to cooking supper," she said. Later I found I could put my hand in his pocket without feeling anxious. He thought I was after his money, but he soon knew better. When I told Felix what I was doing he was pleased and flattered."

Margaret zoomed up her hierarchy. Each step Margaret took up her scale without feeling anxious meant that all the remaining items seemed much less frightening.

Most people, especially those with vague, general anxieties about sex, will need to move more slowly than Margaret. Just touch someone momentarily with your fingertips when you are feeling aroused, and then stop until you feel your anxiety is all the way down to zero. (Fantasy, masturbation, making out, and erotic reading are all useful aids in quelling anxiety and getting you back down to zero.) Take gradual steps. Take them slowly. The next time maybe you can do it a bit longer and maybe you can feel a little more comfortable, but always stop if you have anxiety and go back to zero, until you can touch or kiss or lick or whatever without feeling anxiety. Then go on to the next step in your anxiety hierarchy.

Here are three more examples of anxiety hierarchies, using pleasure as an anxiety fighter.

JACKIE, THIRTY-SEVEN-YEAR-OLD PSYCHIATRIST. She felt that she was too thin, that her body was angular and ugly. We did several things to improve the way she saw herself. We also drew up the following nudity hierarchy.

NUDITY HIERARCHY

0   Lying in bed, relaxed, wearing bra and panties.
10   Lying in bed nude with her partner, under the covers.
20   Lying in bed nude with her partner, no covers, lights off.
40   Gradually taking off her bra and panties, lights on.
50   Lying nude next to her partner. Lights on.
60   Walking around room nude.
70   Partner aroused, admiring her body.

Stay at the lowest step on your hierarchy until you are entirely comfortable and relaxed about doing it. Each step should be a small one as you use arousal and repetition, keeping the pace well under your own control.

It is essential to ban *all* of the other steps on your hierarchy above the one you are working on. Doing them before you reach them on your hierarchy will probably increase your anxiety.

CARRIE, THIRTY-FOUR-YEAR-OLD EDITOR. Carrie was anxious about the sight of her lover's penis. Here, as an example of small, gradual steps, is how she was able to overcome her anxiety. First, she read erotic passages from a novel until she was sexually aroused. Then she repeated each step until she felt no anxiety with that step.

STEP 1:   Write the word *penis*. Write it again. Look at the word. Write it a few more times.

STEP 2:   Say "penis" to herself. Say it again and again.

STEP 3:   Say "penis" out loud.

STEP 4:   Look at a picture of a penis.

STEP 5:   Sit across the room from her partner and imagine his penis underneath his trousers.

STEPS 6–10: Gradually approach his penis. Touch it lightly. Notice the texture, the warmth, the unique combination of softnesses and hardnesses. Treat it as an adventure into an unknown territory without a map. The slower you go, the more you will learn.

CATHERINE, THIRTY-YEAR-OLD FASHION MODEL. Catherine had the following hierarchy for her anxiety about the physical intimacy of sex. It's important to note that Catherine did not go beyond her first step, kissing on the lips, for two weeks, until she felt completely comfortable and relaxed with a simple kiss. She used her own erotic feelings and the relaxation exercise at the end of this chapter to overcome her anxiety, one very small step at a time.

APPROACH HIERARCHY

10   Kissing on the lips.

20   Kissing with tongues.

30   Having her breasts touched through clothing.

40   Being touched above the waist with no clothes on.

50   Touching her partner's genitals through his clothes.

60   Manual stimulation through clothing from her partner.

70   Manual stimulation nude.

80   About to have intercourse.

90   Intercourse.

100 Oral sex.

Partners aren't always as responsive as Margaret's husband, Felix, or as patient or as available as you might wish. And you may feel less than relaxed about asking your partner to help you, at this stage at least, with exercises designed to lower your sexual anxiety ("Lower your what?"). After all, what you want to do is lose your anxiety, not generate more by explaining to a skeptic something you've just read in a book. What I'm leading up to is the anxiety-reducing exercise called graduated calming (desensitization). It's a very strong technique. And you can do it by yourself, because you use your imagination to create the scenes and actions that make you anxious. Strange, but proven true: if you can imagine a scene or action that usually causes you to feel mild anxiety at the same time that you are in a state of deep relaxation, you can unlearn the anxiety. Relaxation competes with anxiety; you can't feel both deep relaxation and intense anxiety at the same time. In graduated calming, relaxation replaces anxiety and breaks the link between anxiety and the action.

Graduated Calming

The more you can relax, the more you can move away from anxiety. Which is why a special relaxation exercise, called deep muscle relaxation, is often an important first step in graduated calming. Deep muscle relaxation is a way of relaxing more deeply than you usually do. It's somewhat repetitious, and it does take practice. So rather than teach you the exercise right here (and leave you too relaxed to continue reading), I've put the detailed instructions in a special section at the end of the chapter. Suffice it to say now that deep muscle relaxation makes you feel wonderfully at ease and relaxed.

Here's how deep muscle relaxation and graduated calming helped one woman overcome a persistent anxiety.

JULIE, TWENTY-SIX-YEAR-OLD INVESTMENT COUNSELOR. Julie had a brave, prim style. She was expensively dressed in tweeds and silk. "It's a bad joke," she said. "I am, I think, a fairly sophisticated person. My job is to tell people how to invest their hard-earned money. That's not something you do lightly. I am anything but sexually naive. Except I have this terror of being penetrated. I cannot bear it. I get very aroused when I make out but as soon as I sense that intercourse is about to begin, I get scared. My mother once hinted that intercourse was something that hurts. I've had intercourse several times with Tommy, my fiancé. He thought it was wonderful. But I hated it. We are going to be married. And I, logically, think that sex ought to be one of the best parts of being married. Logic, I guess, doesn't have much to do with it. I know it's irrational, but I cannot possibly understand how women can allow themselves to be punctured like that."

Julie's plea for help came from real pain. The world was celebrating multiple orgasms and feminine liberation, and she felt like a freakish, lonely outsider. Her pain was both emotional and physical. Tension blocks excitement, and to attempt intercourse before being fully aroused and without adequate lubrication can be painful. Julie needed to feel less anxiety so she could feel pleasure instead of pain. I mention Julie here because of her strong, positive response to graduated calming.

First, deep muscle relaxation was a tremendous boon to Julie outside the bedroom. She had an unusually tense job. Nobody really knows what is going to happen next in the stock market or what the price of copper will be in a year. And yet people gamble millions and hold Julie, in part anyway, responsible. With deep muscle relaxation she could feel the tension float away, leaving her mind clear and sharp. She also found, as many people do, that it was a good way to go to sleep at night, that by relaxing her body she could fall into a deep sleep in a couple of minutes, instead of the hour or so it usually took her to unwind.

In specifically dealing with her fears of being "punctured," I asked Julie to draw up a list and rate its items on a hierarchy scale of anxiety.

JULIE'S ANXIETY HIERARCHY

0   Deep muscle relaxation.

10   Masturbating.

20   Petting with Tom, fully clothed. His hand presses her
            skirt down between her legs.

30   Inserting her finger inside her vagina.

40   Tom touches her bare thighs.

50   Tom suggests they make love.

60   Lying naked on the carpet with Tom. He puts his
            hand between her legs.

75   He puts his finger in her vagina.

85–95   He rubs the outside of her vagina with his penis.

100   Tom enters her.

When Julie was in a state of deep relaxation, I gradually led her up her hierarchy, always repeating, always using deep muscle relaxation to return to zero, until she could in turn imagine each step without feeling anxiety.

Any stress you feel during graduated calming is counterproductive. So you should be very conservative in drawing up your anxiety hierarchy. If you are not sure whether to assign a scene a thirty or a fifty, by all means give it a fifty. Because if you experience a high level of anxiety while you are deeply relaxed, it will destroy your relaxed state. And, equally important, graduated calming works one step at a time. Go up the scale gradually, cautiously, over a period of time. The relaxation inhibits anxiety. But relaxation can inhibit your anxiety only if you keep your anxiety low. To conquer your large anxieties you must first conquer your small ones. Conquering small anxieties generally has the effect of diminishing the larger ones. Conquer a ten, and a ninety tends to move down to eighty.

Here's how you might go through graduated calming yourself. First, relax with the deep-muscle-relaxation instructions at the end of this chapter. In order to do graduated calming you have to be completely relaxed, at zero, so that your relaxation will be strong enough to compete with and win out over your anxiety. Be sure you are in a comfortable, quiet place, where you will not be interrupted. You may find low lights and soft music helpful. When you are perfectly relaxed, at zero, imagine as clearly and with as much detail as possible something that is very low on your scale, say ten or twenty. Imagine that scene for about twenty seconds (or until you begin to feel any anxiety). Then erase the image and relax until you get back to zero. You might like to have a pleasant, relaxing thought to help you return to zero, to replace the thought that causes anxiety. Julie liked to think of sitting on a deck chair, on a porch at a summer cottage, at the beach, with a piña colada in her hand, feeling the warm sun on her and seeing the sky go from bronze to violet in the sunset. Other examples of a pleasant, relaxing thought might be a tall pine tree or a kite fluttering in the sky, or riding in a hot-air balloon on a hot summer day, or the applause after you've starred in a play.

Here are some other aids in getting back down to zero: Exhale slowly, saying the word "calm." Count your fingers without moving them or looking at them. Focus on the texture beneath your fingers without moving them. Count your toes without moving or looking at them. Get a sense of where your knees are without looking at them or touching them. Picture your forehead as being perfectly smooth without any lines or wrinkles. Focus your attention on your knuckles or your ankles without looking at them. When you get back down to zero again (and take as much time as you need to get there), relax, and stay there a few moments.

Next, return to that same thought that is ten or twenty on your hierarchy. Should you feel the first hint of anxiety, erase the thought, and go back to deep relaxation. You will need to repeat that scene.

The point is to repeat the process until the scene does not cause you any anxiety. When you can imagine the scene without any anxiety, continue to imagine it for about twenty seconds. Hold it for another five or ten seconds, and savor how relaxed you feel. Then erase the scene.

When you no longer feel anxiety during the scene that is ten or twenty on your scale, you can move up to the next scene, the one you labeled twenty or thirty. Always be careful to cut off the image as soon as you feel the least bit anxious, and do not repeat the thought until you are back at zero, deeply relaxed. And always be careful to move up only ten or, at the most, twenty points on the scale for the next scene. Be sure that relaxation always wins and anxiety always loses, so that relaxation is learned and anxiety is unlearned.

Each time Julie was able to imagine a scene that once caused anxiety without feeling anxious, she was able to experience in real life what she imagined without anxiety. And she was able to feel sexual pleasure. When Julie, in a state of deep relaxation, could imagine Tom putting his penis inside her — when she could picture the scene that used to make her feel terrified, trapped, and the victim of violence — when she could imagine that scene with equanimity, feeling quite relaxed, she could also enjoy making love with Tom in reality.

Let's look quickly at another example.

BANNING, FIFTY-TWO-YEAR-OLD PHYSICIAN. When Banning was fifteen her mother caught her masturbating. Her mother screamed at her and told her she was committing a "dirty, nasty, immoral act." Banning said that was the only time she had heard her mother discuss sex. Banning developed anxiety about experiencing any sexual pleasure.

BANNING'S SEXUAL PLEASURE/ANXIETY
HIERARCHY

10 Banning's husband expresses sexual pleasure.

20 She feels sexual desire.

30 She feels sexual pleasure. (Something her mother said she shouldn't feel.)

50 Expressing sexual pleasure, saying "that feels good," moaning.

60 She feels sexual pleasure from oral stimulation.

70 Intense sexual pleasure, close to an orgasm.

90 Having an orgasm.

When Banning was able to imagine herself feeling intense sexual pleasure with her husband, without any anxiety, she found that she could also feel intense sexual pleasure with her husband in the bedroom.

There are other ways of dealing with anxiety: assertiveness, seduction, intimate communication (asking, talking, laughing), and more knowledge about how you do certain things. These are covered in later chapters.

Sometimes having sex at a different time, or changing the order of sexual play, or making love in a different place can sidestep anxiety (see chapter 12, "A Sensual Holiday").

Sharing your vulnerabilities, simply letting your anxieties out in the open, instead of grimly enduring them in silence, can diminish them. Because assertiveness, expressing your feelings, inhibits anxiety. One woman, for example, lowered her anxiety to a barely noticeable "five" simply by saying, "I'm really scared. I'm not very good at this." A man, by telling his partner "Sometimes I take a long time to come. I hope you don't mind," was able to take the pressure off himself to "perform."

One way to reduce anxiety that I especially like is thinking of sex as an adventure — as if you were the first explorer in America. There are no maps. Keep your ears, eyes, and other sensory antennae alert. It's a whole new country every time, and you don't know what you'll find. That attitude implies a certain amount of bravery, and a willingness to endure a few stray arrows from the blind emotional side. But an attitude of adventure can lead you to some amazing discoveries — mountains of pleasure where you had expected only calm sea — as long as you do it gradually, in a warm and loving context.

Finally, there may still be some small anxiety. Particularly if you are with someone new, or trying out something new.

Sex is our venture into the wild. Always there are new, untried things. Always the slightest new sound or smell is a surprise. Sexual confidence is keeping your senses keen, as you are listening, tasting, and testing, one step at a time, alert to your life and another life amazingly close to yours.

EXERCISES

Deep Relaxation

First, a demonstration to give you an idea of how deep muscle relaxation works:

I want you to make a fist, and tighten all the muscles in your right arm. Make the muscles as tight and as hard as you can, so that your arm is as rigid as you can make it. Notice all the sensations in your arm and concentrate on the muscle tension in your biceps. Now I want you to let go gradually, relax your arm slowly, and notice how that "letting go" is an activity itself. It is the uncontracting of your muscles. Keep on letting go until your arm feels totally relaxed. I say "feels" totally relaxed because, although most of the muscle fibers in your arm feel relaxed, some of the muscles will still be contracted. So keep on letting go. Try to continue that letting go activity beyond the point of simple relaxation and deeply relax all the muscles in your arm. Notice the feeling in your arm.

Now clench your fist again and make your whole arm as rigid as iron. Make it as tight as you possibly can and become aware of what your arm feels like. Keep on being aware of that feeling as you begin to relax. See if you can picture the muscles in your arm as you totally relax your arm. Let your arm relax even more. If you concentrate all of your attention on your arm, you will find some few muscle fibers are still tense. It is the relaxation of those additional fibers that will bring about deep relaxation. So repeat the process of slowly tightening and relaxing your arm, being aware of the muscles in your arm and observing them as they relax, and when you feel your arm completely relaxed, see if you can go beyond that furthest point and relax still further. Try to go beyond what seems to be the furthest point.

That's a fair example of deep muscle relaxation, a systematic way of driving out tension by letting your mind become aware of and relaxing each part of your body in turn, by concentrating on that part of your body, feeling any muscles that might be tense and letting them go.

Deep muscle relaxation requires that you become physically passive. Yet you remain an alert observer and reporter of your own body's degree of relaxation.

Most people can't fully relax on their first try. Deep relaxation has to be learned, and it does take practice. So while fifteen or twenty minutes of relaxation may, at first, just relax your forearm, eventually you'll be able to relax your whole body in a minute or two. On the other hand, you might just be one of those lucky people who, on the very first attempt at deep relaxation, experiences deepening and extending relaxation radiating throughout your body, and feels general effects such as calmness, sleepiness, or warmth. The effect that you want to achieve is a peaceful state, in which you feel no tension, no anxiety, no worries, no negative emotions whatsoever.

If you have access to a tape recorder, you might like to record the next section in an easy, relaxed voice. And then whenever you want to practice deep muscle relaxation, listen to the tape. You'll find it's a great help because, with the tape recorder giving you instructions, your mind will be free to follow and find the muscles that need relaxing.

Find a comfortable, quiet place, where you know you won't be disturbed. Now make yourself comfortable by lying down or stretching out on a sofa, or sitting back in an easy chair. Then, with your arms at your sides and your legs straight out, with your feet slightly apart, relax.

Erase the thoughts of the things that happened today. Make your mind a perfect blank. Let go of all your worries and hopes and fears — feel your mind float free in space. Now be aware of your left leg. Picture the muscles and bones in your left leg. Lift your left leg six inches and tighten all the muscles in your left leg . . . tighter and tighter until it is rigid. Now all at once, let go of all the muscles in your left leg and let it drop. Roll it slowly from side to side a couple of times, to be sure all the muscles are completely relaxed. Just let it lie there, totally relaxed. Now bring your mind's awareness to your right leg. Picture the muscles and bones inside. Lift the leg six inches, tighten all your right-leg muscles until they are rigid, keep your leg rigid for a couple of moments, then drop it, roll it from side to side, completely relaxed, and forget it.

Now bring your mind to your left arm. Concentrate on the muscles and bones in your left arm. Lift it six inches in the air and tighten all the muscles as hard as you can. Tighten harder. Then let the arm drop. Roll it from side to side a couple of times, to make sure your arm is completely relaxed, and then forget it.

Now tighten your buttocks. Squeeze as hard as you can, hold them, tighter, now let go and relax. Inhale so that your stomach pushes out as far as it will go. Squeeze in another breath so that it expands farther. Hold it. Now exhale — let it go all at once and forget it. Relax.

Bring your awareness to your chest and shoulders. Lift your shoulders up and, with your arms completely relaxed, tighten your shoulder and chest muscles as if you were trying to touch your shoulders in front of you. Tighter. Now let your shoulders drop. Relax.

Now picture all the muscles in your neck and tighten them. Tighten them so hard that the cords in your neck stand out. Tighter. Let go all at once. Relax. Roll your head gently from side to side, to be sure all the neck muscles are relaxed.

Now squeeze your face muscles as if you were trying to bring all of the features of your face to one point around your nose. Make your face as tight and pursed as if it were becoming a prune. Now let go.

Take a deep breath and hold it. Open your eyes and your

mouth as wide as you can. Stick your tongue out as far as it will go. Open your eyes and your mouth wider so you can feel your face stretch. Stick your tongue out farther. Now all at once, let out your breath and relax your face. Relax.

Your body should be completely relaxed. Let your mind cruise down to your left and your right legs, your left arm and your right arm, your stomach, buttocks, shoulders, chest, neck, and face in turn, to be sure that all the muscles in your body are peaceful and relaxed. Search out any tension that may remain in any muscle, and let go of that muscle. Let it relax still further. Allow yourself enough time to go slowly over your body and ease any tension that may still remain. You might feel drowsy or warm or a kind of pleasant tingling. Feel how good it feels to be calm and relaxed.

You can become twice as relaxed as you are merely by taking in a really deep breath and slowly exhaling. With your eyes closed (so that you become less aware of objects and movements around you and can thus prevent any surface tensions from developing), breathe in deeply and feel yourself becoming heavier. Take in a long, deep breath and let it out very slowly. Feel how heavy and relaxed you have become. Some people find they can deepen their relaxation further by mentally reviewing the parts of their bodies and saying to themselves, "My foot [or calf or thigh or whatever] is limp and warm and heavy." This should be done slowly, repeating each statement once or twice so your body has time to respond to your instructions.

In a state of perfect relaxation you should feel unwilling to move a single muscle in your body. Think about the effort that would be required to raise your right arm. As you think about raising your right arm, see if you can notice any tensions that might have crept into your shoulder and your arm.

Now you decide not to lift the arm but to continue relaxing. Observe the relief and the disappearance of the tension.

Keep on relaxing like that. When you wish to get up, count

backward from four to one. You should then feel fine and refreshed, wide awake and calm.

So that is deep muscle relaxation. Practice it twice a day (in bed at night before going to sleep is a good time, because it will also help you get to sleep) until you can do it easily.

Once you've done two weeks of deep muscle relaxation twice daily, you may well not have to tense your muscles before you relax them. Focusing on observing and relaxing without preliminary tensing will help you to relax in a shorter time.

6

Unlearning Jealousy

THE FIRST NONVIOLENT CURE

One anxiety has a marked potential for violence — jealousy.

Jealousy is pain in action, moving, searching, looking for a place to land. Sooner or later, everyone suffers from it. Its pain is universal.

Jealousy is a powerful and primitive obsession. Consider how it can kill the pleasures of a summer afternoon with random, growing suspicion. Consider how it blocks creativity or even the ability to leave the house to pick up the laundry ("As soon as I leave, she'll call him here. I *know* she will"). Jealousy blocks sexual feelings ("Stop that! I want to know where you were this afternoon"). Many murders and violent attacks are inflicted not on strangers but on wives and husbands, lovers and suspected lovers, victims of jealousy. Men who have never cried before have called me on the phone weeping with jealousy, asking for help.

There are degrees of jealousy, of course, ranging from mild twinges to obsessive waves of rage that block all other thoughts or cares or possibilities. It is never a compliment ("I'm jealous just because I love you so much" is simply its most common excuse). But it always erodes your confidence.

In *How to Fall Out of Love,* I outlined in detail a nonviolent cure for jealousy. There, I was dealing with a love that is not returned. Here I'd like to expand that theme to include all kinds of jealousy.

Even when jealousy is justified, it is still destructive to the person who feels it. It may be that the relationship itself is not viable. It may be that the only cure is to leave that relationship. But in most cases, you don't have to take so drastic a step. In most cases there is a way to reduce the pain of jealousy and make it much more manageable.

Jealousy is learned. You may have learned it in your very earliest days, before you could speak, before you can remember. Perhaps a neighbor stopped by for a cup of coffee while your mother was playing with you in your crib, and your mother stopped playing with you to enjoy a few minutes of welcome adult conversation. You howled and screamed, and your mother shut the door, leaving you to scream to yourself. Possibly your father lured your mother away every evening when he came home. Possibly when you first went to kindergarten you found others getting more attention than you did. Possibly your mother came home one day with a new baby, and her love was no longer all yours. However you first learned jealousy, you know what it feels like. When someone you love gives his or her time and attention to someone else, it feels like rejection. There's no way you can prepare for rejection. Sometimes it's so powerful that it's overwhelming.

Yes, you know that jealousy is unreasonable. And you know that you can't possibly have all of another person's time and affection, and that even if you could, you wouldn't want it. You know your lover needs other friends, other interests, and time to be alone. You know that jealousy makes you ugly and weak. But the monster accepts no reasons — except the ones that feed your suspicions.

EDNA, THIRTY-EIGHT-YEAR-OLD TEACHER. There was a small college in the Virginia town where Edna grew up. And it was there that she met Harmon. "Harmon wasn't just the most popular man on campus, he was the nicest." After graduate school, Harmon returned to the college as an instructor in the English department. He and Edna were married right after her graduation. Harmon is now a professor. Friendly, confident, with a warm smile and a good listening ear, Harmon has a tremendous number of friends. Many of his colleagues and students are women. Women confide in Harmon, and they ask his advice. "I know he has commitments, that a lot of the people he has to see are women," said Edna, "but I am sick, I mean physically sick, with jealousy. I understand about my insecure childhood, I know I'm too darn possessive, but understanding the reasons is not enough. If I overhear that so and so saw Harmon having lunch with some woman, there is a fifty-fifty chance I'll be sick or have an awful headache or both. Harmon is a fine man, and he is good and kind and considerate to me. But after all these years, I'm not getting better, I'm getting worse. Jealousy interferes with my work and my kids, and my house is a mess. I'm exhausted and I hate myself. I'm a strong woman. But I'm not strong enough to endure this anymore. It's gotten so that the only time I don't feel jealous of him is when we're making love or we're off on a trip together.

"I really do not believe Harmon is having sexual relations with other women. What terrifies me, though, is the feeling he's going to leave me."

Edna had flown in to see me. We spent the next three days in an intensive concentrated program. First I taught her the techniques of thought stopping (see chapter 3), so that when her husband was going to have lunch with a woman, Edna could stop brooding about it. We also drew up a list of "reasonable requests" that Edna would make of Harmon:

1. That he not tell Edna of his attraction or admiration for women he happened to see.
2. That he have lunch with other women one to two times a week instead of two to three times.

3. That he talk to Edna just before and just after lunch with another woman.

The technique we spent the most time on, the most effective technique against jealousy, was graduated calming. (That's the technique from chapter 5 that uses deep muscle relaxation and your imagination, and helps you overcome anxiety step by step. Jealousy is a negative emotion, like anxiety, and the treatment is the same.)

Edna was very tired and tense. Learning deep muscle relaxation, learning how to relax more than she had ever done before, was, in her words, "better than a week at a beauty farm." Organizing and writing down her jealous feelings was helpful, too. She could see what was bothering her and how much. Here is Edna's jealousy hierarchy.

EDNA'S JEALOUSY HIERARCHY

0   Edna imagines she is sitting in a beautiful green field on the side of a mountain. She hears cowbells in the distance. Across the valley, beyond the river, there is a high mountain range. Above the snow-covered peaks, blue sky and white clouds.

20   Harmon describes his favorite actress in sexy detail.

35   Harmon admires a woman on the street.

55   Harmon has lunch with another woman and tells Edna about the lunch.

65   He's talking to a woman on the phone. He's animated, gregarious, listening intently, giving advice, telling stories.

80   Edna hears from someone else about his having lunch with a woman.

90   He has dinner with a woman.

100 Edna imagines he's fallen in love with someone else and deserts Edna. She feels she has failed in the marriage.

Edna's pain was so deep and strong that I wondered if those three days had been enough.

She called ten days later:

"It's delicious. We went to a small party. He moved around, talked to everybody, like he does. And it was O.K. For the first time in my life it was O.K. I just grinned like a cat."

A month later she called again:

"Harmon's flown to New York for a conference. He's done all the things on our list. Except abandon me for another woman. And I have to tell you I feel so calm and relaxed." The thought of Harmon's leaving her, the scenes of lunches and phone calls had all dropped down to a fraction of their former intensity.

Let me give you some other examples, some unusual and some more common. Note how the items on your hierarchy can be either things that are real or things you imagine.

MARIA, THIRTY-FOUR-YEAR-OLD RECEPTIONIST. Her husband worked in a large insurance office. Maria knew he was surrounded by attractive women. She also imagined he had affairs.

MARIA'S JEALOUSY HIERARCHY.

20   Her husband surrounded by attractive women at work.

35   He has a business lunch with a woman.

50   Her husband goes on a business trip.

65   She imagines her husband having drinks with another woman on the trip.

80   She imagines him having dinner with another woman on the trip.

95   She imagines him making love to another woman in Atlanta, in Los Angeles, or in Chicago.

JOANNE, FORTY-SEVEN-YEAR-OLD ART DIRECTOR. Joanne is married for the second time. Her husband, Charles, has also been married before. He had also had several affairs before marrying Joanne. His past haunts her.

JOANNE'S JEALOUSY HIERARCHY

25 The thought of her husband's secretary. (He once slept with her.)

35 The thought of his administrative assistant (who is in love with Joanne's husband).

50 The former lovers he still occasionally sees.

65 He has lunch with his most recent former lover.

75 He sees his former wife in Grand Central Station and they have a long, seemingly intimate conversation.

MAL, TWENTY-EIGHT-YEAR-OLD RESTAURANT OWNER. Mal and Sharon, the woman he lived with for five years, were swingers. They were into group sex and swapping partners.

They always did things together. And they faithfully told each other when there was going to be another liaison. One place was sacrosanct, a beach house they reserved just for themselves, no guests, no swinging, just themselves on a romantic weekend. One afternoon, Sharon came home early from her office job and found Mal in bed with a woman. Furious, she told him she had spent an evening with a friend of his at their hideaway beach house. Mal went berserk. He screamed and yelled, and from then on he had to know where Sharon spent every moment of her day. She told him but he never believed her.

MAL'S JEALOUSY HIERARCHY

0 Calm, deeply relaxed.

20 Sharon is late for dinner.

30 Sharon calls to say she is having an office party and will be home late.

45   Sharon comes home with her blouse and skirt rumpled.

60   Mal notices Sharon has beach sand in her shoes.

90   Sharon has sex with another man at the beach house.

100   Sharon tells Mal she doesn't want to see him anymore.

ADRIENNE, TWENTY-SIX-YEAR-OLD PHARMACOLOGIST.

ADRIENNE'S JEALOUSY HIERARCHY

0   She imagines she is floating down a placid river on a sunny autumn afternoon, watching the reflections of the brilliant autumn leaves in the water.

25   Someone tells her that David, her boyfriend, was seen having a drink with another woman.

30   She sees David drive by with another woman in the front seat.

45   At a party she sees David talking intensely to another woman.

60   At a party she sees David dancing with another woman.

80   At a party she sees David kissing another woman.

100   At a party, looking for David, she finds him in the bedroom with another woman.

MAX, SEVENTEEN-YEAR-OLD HIGH-SCHOOL STUDENT.

MAX'S JEALOUSY HIERARCHY

0   He is fishing on a lazy morning in May.

40   His girlfriend looks at another boy.

50   His girlfriend talks to another boy.

80   His girlfriend calls up another boy.

100   His girlfriend goes out on a date with another boy.

Max's hierarchy started at such an intense level of jealousy that it took us a while to find a scene with his girlfriend in which he was just a little jealous. In going over their school day together, we found that Max sitting in homeroom class with his girlfriend, when there were other boys in the room, was about ten; Max and his girlfriend walking down the hall together between classes was about twenty; his girlfriend walking down the hall alone when there were other boys present was about thirty.

After four weeks, Max could see his girlfriend talking to other boys and not feel jealous.

High levels of jealousy aren't so rare as you might suppose. Jealousy feeds on itself. Using graduated calming you cut off its source of nourishment. It takes repetition, and it takes time. But graduated calming is the first and, as far as I know, only nonviolent cure for jealousy.

As I've mentioned, it is fairly certain that sooner or later you will have to deal with jealousy. Now, before this negative emotion grows to destructive proportions, you have the means to overcome it.

EXERCISES

Deep Muscle Relaxation

1. Practice deep muscle relaxation, as described in chapter 5, two times a day.

2. Also, focus on relaxing a small area, such as your neck or your forearm, for five minutes every day.

3. Every time you pick up a telephone, sit down to eat, or come to a stoplight or stop sign or crosswalk, take a brief few seconds to focus on relaxing a finger, knee, biceps, or other small part of your body, to help integrate relaxation into your life.

4. Once you've done two weeks of deep muscle relaxation twice daily, you may well not have to tense your muscles before you relax them. Focusing on observing and relaxing without preliminary tensing will help you to relax in a shorter time.

Graduated Calming

1. Relax until you are at zero on your jealousy hierarchy.

2. Bring on or imagine the first scene from your hierarchy.

3. If you feel *any* jealousy, erase the scene.

4. Go back to relaxing until you get to zero.

5. Bring the scene on again and continue imagining it, but, again, if you feel any jealousy erase the scene.

6. Go back to relaxing until you get to zero.

7. When you can continue imagining the scene for about

twenty seconds and still feel yourself so relaxed that you stay at zero, savor how relaxed you feel with this scene. Then erase it.

8. Continue relaxing.

9. Continue the whole process (at a later time, if you wish) with the next scene on your hierarchy.

PART TWO

LEARNING

═══════════

Just for now, put aside the way you usually make love . . .

There is so much to learn.

7

Learning Strength

Who is that talking? Whose is that familiar and yet somehow off-key voice? Hearing your own voice for the first time on a tape recorder is a strange and unsettling experience.

You have the feeling that the tape recorder is wrong. Your voice is different, has a different pitch, another resonance. Then you realize that the way you hear yourself is one thing, and the way others hear you is different.

Television has something of the same effect. For years you've seen yourself, you imagine, quite clearly. And yet seeing yourself on TV for the first time is a jolt. That person identified as you looks something like you, is wearing the same clothes, and yet there are differences. Again you realize that the way you see yourself is different from the way others see you.

Your self-image — the way you view your appearance, emotions, opinions, strengths, and weaknesses — is probably your single most important view of reality. The tape recorder or the TV camera may offer you one slightly jarring image of yourself, but that, as you know, is only one facet of yourself. As your own self-camera, you have a multi-lens view that includes your past, your hopes for the future, your worries, and your moods, to mention just some of the data that color and shape your self-image. As a key to the way people treat you, and the way you treat yourself, the way you see yourself is crucial.

A negative self-image — being down on yourself — makes you unhappy, gets in the way of almost anything worthwhile you want to do, and is generally unrealistic. Unfortunately, it's also pretty common. Most people have an unrealistic and unduly pessimistic view of themselves.

Perhaps it's just human nature to focus on negatives. Perhaps it's because a large part of your self-image comes from the negatives of other people: friends, parents, teachers, lovers, bosses, coworkers, whose criticism can be destructive of your self-esteem. Parents scold, correct, and chastise their children. Husbands tell their wives they shouldn't do this or that. Wives tell their husbands that they're fools for trying to do that or this. And we live in a culture that holds up impossible models. The media, with their stereotypes of perfection, seem to encourage us to take a dim view of ourselves.

SEEING YOURSELF IN A BETTER MIRROR: IMPROVING YOUR BODY IMAGE

False idols, called fashion models and movie and TV stars, distort your self-view to make you think you should be shorter or taller or thinner, or have bigger or smaller feet, breasts, hands, eyes, genitalia. An industry called fashion keeps otherwise sane people running after a "look" that is temporarily "now," and probably dated by the time we mortals don the costume of the moment.

Throughout this book you have been learning to see yourself differently. In unlearning anxieties, guilts, and old ties, you have been removing some of the destructive images that darken the way you look at yourself.

Now I'd like to suggest additional ways of strengthening your self-image. I'm not arguing for rose-colored glasses or simple optimism. But you can change the angle and focus of your self-vision so that your "faults" don't loom quite so large in the foreground and your strengths stand out in the open, where there is room for them to grow.

It's often assumed that women are the ones who are most dissatisfied with their bodies. The burden has been on them to be "pretty," "shapely," "sexy," after the fashion of today's male fantasies. Yet a recent study indicates that men are far from immune from wishing their bodies were different. For example, many men wish they had a larger penis. This wish comes from the dinosaur myth that "bigger is better." It also comes from their point of view: looking straight down, they see their penis foreshortened, whereas looking across the locker room, they see other men's penises as if they were longer than theirs, owing to the more horizontal angle of vision.

While I cannot help you change your body, I can help you see yourself from a more realistic angle. I can help you appreciate some of the stronger, more positive aspects of your appearance.

If you learn to like your body, you can learn to use it as an instrument of pleasure, both for yourself and for your partner. When you feel good about touching your body and moving your body and seeing your body, as opposed to just "having" a body, you can bring so much more pleasure into your life — pleasure in small, everyday gestures (dressing and undressing can become a pleasure rather than an everyday chore), and pleasure upon pleasure in making love.

The first step to take toward liking your body is to call into question your own "objective" point of view. It might be that the way you see yourself isn't very accurate.

SUSAN, THIRTY-THREE-YEAR-OLD MOTHER OF THREE. Susan was generally considered by her friends to be the reigning beauty at the tennis club. She had auburn hair, a peaches-and-cream complexion, beautiful blue eyes, and a slim and graceful figure. She told me "I'm not satisfied with my body. I don't like the shape of my breasts. I won't wear a bathing suit. I haven't worn one in five years. And my complexion is too fair."

One antidote for Susan, and perhaps for you, is to listen for and accept compliments. When people tell you that they like the way you look or the way you are dressed, say "Thank you." Say "I'm really glad you like the way I look." Accepting compliments instead of dismissing them ("Oh, I've gained six pounds." "I've had this dress for years." "It was a bargain special") helps you begin to accept a viewpoint that is probably more objective than your own.

JERRY, THIRTY-NINE-YEAR-OLD LAWYER. If beauty is in the eye of the beholder, so are flaws. Jerry had always felt he was too short. "Look at our cultural heroes," he said. "They're football and basketball players. The Marlboro man is a tall man." I pointed out to Jerry that the man voted most sexy in a recent survey was Woody Allen, a gentleman widely noted for wit, not height.

I suggested to Jerry that he write down at least two positive things about his appearance every day. Positives can be a kind of general praise ("I'm good-looking") or more specific ("My complexion is good"). Praise the hair on your chest, the tone of your calf muscle. Praise yourself for exercising, for not eating fattening foods, for having beautiful eyes.

"You can also praise yourself for things unrelated to your appearance," I told Jerry, "because that helps strengthen your self-image in general. It also takes your focus away from your looks."

Praising yourself is powerful and assertive. It inhibits your anxiety and tends to give you a more positive picture of yourself. As you act stronger, you see that you are stronger. As people see you act more assertively, they are more likely to respect you. Being assertive, you are more likely to get what you want and be who you'd like to be.

So now the point is to encourage yourself (by praising

yourself) to start moving toward positive actions that have some degree of assertiveness ("I told Max how I want those reports done." "I laid out my theory of commodities for Penny." "I moved the furniture so it looks better." "I fixed the door"). Be generous. Praise yourself. And praise yourself every day in writing for six weeks.

The next step is to take a little time, while you are relaxed, for a brief survey of your body. Bear in mind the prayer "O God, give us serenity to accept what cannot be changed, courage to change what should be changed, and wisdom to distinguish the one from the other." There may be some things you can change, physically. You can eat less, exercise more, buy contact lenses, play basketball at lunchtime, see a hair stylist or a plastic surgeon. But the real key is the way you see yourself. If only you could see yourself as a lover sees you! The best guide is someone who is in love with you, taking you on a slow survey of your body, stopping off from time to time at the points of interest and beauty.

It's a trip you can and should take yourself. Remember the goal here is not to compete with a fashion model, movie star, or acquaintance. The goal is not to compete with anybody, not even yourself. What you need is to simply accept yourself, to recognize your strengths and be kind to your imperfections.

So sit back or lie down, relax, and take a quiet, leisurely cruise from the top of your head to the tips of your toes. As you travel, pay particular attention to every part that pleases you along the way. Describe to yourself everything you like about your body, such as your complexion or the shape of your eyes, the strong line of your nose or chin, or the muscles in your calf. You can also include things you can't see — like the sound of your laugh or the strength in your hands.

Accepting yourself, feeling at ease and relaxed about the way you look, is far more attractive than any physical characteristic. The movers and shakers of history, the leaders of the world who exercise power and wield great charm, are rarely noted for their pretty bodies. Albert Einstein, Sigmund Freud, Eleanor Roosevelt, Andy Warhol, Henry Kissinger, Anwar Sadat, Menachem Begin, Margaret Mead, John Kenneth Galbraith, Elton John, Robert McNamara, Golda Meir, John Lennon, Indira Gandhi, Telly Savalas, and Marie Curie have very little in common. Except that though they are or were all world-famous, they wouldn't win third prize in a neighborhood beauty contest. At the same time, some of the world's most gorgeous-looking people have told me what a lonely, empty burden it is to be valued solely for their looks.

Beauty is different things to different people. If you assume, for example, that more men are attracted to large breasts than to small breasts, you're probably wrong. An informal survey showed that men were pretty well divided on the subject. Some said they preferred small breasts, some liked medium-sized, and some preferred large breasts. A few said they had no particular preference, because they were more attracted by legs or hands or a smile. Some said they liked all sizes.

So begin at the top of your head and focus on your hair, forehead, eyebrows, temples, cheekbones, the color of your eyes, and the profile of your nose. Compliment yourself every time you can. Do it wholeheartedly, without reservation. If you start saying something critical, STOP. You've been critical of yourself too often as it is. You don't need to reinforce negative images of yourself.

CLAIRE, FORTY-TWO-YEAR-OLD WRITER. Claire was short, round, shy, and lonely. She had a habit of taking her glasses off and rubbing her eyes as if she were tired. "Well, I am tired, tired of myself," she said. "The closest I ever got to glamour was when Richard Burton described Elizabeth Taylor as having a double chin and being short in the leg. That," she said, "is me to a T. Except I have a face that looks more like Burton than Taylor."

Claire's spirits lifted hardly at all when I pointed out that she was taller than the original Queen Cleopatra, Queen Victoria, and Margaret Mead. "I'm also shorter than the tall man at the circus," she said, "which means about as much. Besides, it isn't just my height, I'm bored with my whole dumpy body. I'd like to dump it for a new one. And I hate my breasts," Claire added, sitting up. "I hate my stupid breasts. They're tiny, a quarter of the size they should be. I'd love, just for a week or for a day, I'd love just once to have lovely, full swinging breasts.

I asked Claire to look for and observe beautiful women with small breasts. I also asked Claire to make a mental list of five beautiful women with small breasts. I stressed that she use her own definition of *beautiful*. There are certainly enough women to choose from — women who are in movies, medicine, education, research, law, business, automotive design; friends; acquaintances. Whatever your definition of beautiful, I think you'll find a number of women who have small breasts and are beautiful.

One of the best ways to stop focusing on something you don't like about yourself is to focus on something you do like. I asked Claire to tell me what she did like about her body. She said her nose was O.K., and she had to confess her skin was wonderfully soft, and her legs, while they were, of course, short, were, after all, pretty nice.

Later, as Claire began to stop focusing on her breasts and to take pleasure from her complexion and from seeing her legs as beautiful, she was able to walk into a room with more confidence. Her attitude toward other people softened. As she gained confidence and became more approachable, she began to make some new friends. She became less shy.

OTHER PICTURES OF YOURSELF: ASSERTIVE BEHAVIOR

Sometimes shyness is a self-defense against the possible dangers of social encounters. To some degree, the dangers are real. After all, you might be rejected. Shyness is closely linked to your self-image. If you feel insecure, if you feel that you are unattractive or haven't much to offer, then you are bound to feel a high risk of rejection. You peek over your wall of timidity, hoping for a glimpse of friendship and acceptance — hoping at the same time you won't be seen. At first glance shyness might seem to be an endearing trait. Yet shyness extracts a high price. It is a barrier to intimacy. Afraid to put your best foot forward, you improvise, invent another person to hide behind, blurt out what you never meant to say. Or you say nothing at all.

There are a number of ways to reduce shyness — and all of them come under the heading of being assertive.

Being assertive improves your self-image. Assertive behavior lessens your shyness in an exercise of self. Acting assertively makes it possible for you to feel positive emotions, such as love, more strongly.

Assertiveness is the ability and the emotional freedom to express opinions and feelings with confidence and strength. It is standing up for yourself and not letting others take advantage of you. (The following section on assertiveness and assertive exercises has been adapted from my earlier book, *How to Fall Out of Love*.)

Like other emotions and behaviors, assertiveness is learned. As you learn assertiveness step by step, becoming stronger and less anxious in social situations, your self-image will improve in a direct step-by-step parallel. So you begin in a small way with easy things. Ask someone you know for a small favor, or express an opinion about the weather ("I think it's warm enough"). As commonplace as the opinion may be, it is, for some, an essential trial step. The point is to make it easy on yourself, so that you know you will succeed. Happily, assertiveness also improves the way people think of you. Because if you are assertive, instead of timid or aggressive, if you are self-confident, instead of wishy-washy, you change your environment, as people tend to respond to you more positively. People take advantage of you less and value you more.

Changing your self-image means learning to think more positively about yourself. The negative images you have of yourself may be strong or weak. In either case, they won't be changed just by deciding to change them. Or by just resolving to feel better about yourself in the morning. Changing your self-image takes exercise and practice. You have to relearn on an emotional level. Because the facts don't, won't, and can't change. What you can change is the emotional light in which you see yourself.

Assertive Assignments

Should any exercise cause you any anxiety, tension, or discomfort, don't do it. If you still want to do the exercise, try it out on the cat or dog, or silently in your own mind. And then, once you can imagine it and/or carry it out without discomfort, you can go on to try it out in a more challenging situation. On the other hand, if you feel you are already beyond an exercise, good. Skip it. What you should do is build yourself up by easy steps until you can handle more threatening or negative situations than you could before.

1. *Compliments* (for three weeks or until it is easy). Accept all compliments without downgrading yourself.

Example: Instead of replying "Oh, I got it five years ago as a bargain," say "I'm really glad you like it."

Example: Instead of replying "Anybody could have done it," say "I'm happy you noticed."

2. *Expressing Opinions* (for three weeks or until it is easy). Express two opinions a day. Start with nonthreatening subjects and express them to nonthreatening people, gradually increasing the degree of controversy of the subjects and by degrees expressing yourself to more threatening people. Your opinions can be positive or negative, as long as they are yours. Impor-

tant: You don't have to say how things make you feel, merely what you think.

Example: To a friend, "I think bringing back family movies was a great idea for kids."

Example: To someone you've just met, "I think television sets should be made to face the wall one day a week."

Write down the opinions you express on a card.

3. *Expressing Feelings.* Express one or two feelings a day to one or two people. Begin with easy feelings with friends.

Example: "I'm really glad I met you today."

Example: "I'm so sorry about that."

Example: "Wow." "Sensational." "Outrageous."

Example: "I feel happy when I'm with you."

Don't say anything that makes you uncomfortable. Make sure assertiveness wins over anxiety.

4. *Modeling* (whenever you try any of the exercises and whenever you feel you need extra confidence). Get an image in your mind of someone you think of as very self-confident. Keep that individual in mind as you try to act the way he or she might act. Think of and use the words they would use, their tone of voice, eye contact, and posture.

5. *Say No* (or disagree). If you never or rarely say "no," practice saying "no" at least twice a week when someone asks you to do something you don't want to do. However, if this makes you feel tense, begin by just thinking about saying "no." In either case, write down on a card all the times you think or say "no."

6. *Asking Favors* (once a week). If you are not used to asking for a favor, ask. Begin with a very small favor from someone you know well.

You deserve to be treated with consideration. To earn consideration you have to ask for it. And you will have to practice assertive behavior in order to learn to ask. These exercises are like the basic exercises you do when you learn to swim or play the piano. They stretch and develop new emotional muscles, reduce your anxiety, and help you toward a better self-image.

7. *Buy Something and Return It.* An exercise in getting things your way.

8. *Quiet Table.* Go into a restaurant and insist, firmly but nicely, on a quiet table.

9. *Rehearsal* (then try it out). With a friend or by yourself act out the following situations:

A. You are in line. Someone cuts in front of you. You ask him/her to go to the end of the line.

B. In a restaurant the steak is overdone. Ask the waiter, quietly but firmly, to take it back.

C. At a fancy beach a lifeguard tells you to leave because this is a private beach. Tell the lifeguard the law in the town says there is no such thing as a private beach.

Self-indulgence is a way of giving yourself positive reinforcement. Here are a few suggestions. You may well think of other, better ones. Being good to yourself isn't a luxury, it's a necessity for improving your self-image.

10. *Bed.* Stay in bed an extra three minutes in the morning.

11. *Lotion.* Enjoy the sensation of putting on hand lotion slowly.

12. *If You Can't Think of Anything Good to Do for Yourself.* Think of something good to do for a friend or just call an old friend, or do something good for your house or apartment.

13. *Cats.* Watch how a cat seeks pleasure in each moment. Notice how it seeks out the most comfortable spot in the room. And how it stretches. And how it climbs on you when it wants to be petted. Spend ten minutes like a cat.

14. *One Day* (once a month). Spend one day as if it were your only day. Just today. What would you like to do?

15. *Exercise.* Of course you should. It's easiest if you go to an exercise, dance, or yoga class. But you can also do sit-ups, touch your toes, and jog. It makes your body stronger and your mind function better.

16. *Bubble Bath*. Soak.

Once you have done some of the above exercises, you'll find that it feels easier to meet people. Improving your self-image improves your self-confidence and helps you feel less shy.

"Hello. I've seen you walking by here every morning and I can't help wondering where you're headed." "You look as if you're looking for something. Can I help?"

Sometimes the simplest opening of all is the best.

"Hello."

One beautiful undergraduate started smiling and saying hello in response to smiles and hellos from a young man who passed her on campus every morning. She couldn't help being curious about him and attracted to him. But after reaching the level of "hello" they seemed stuck. She didn't want to seem aggressive; it would have been out of character. Also she sensed that he was as shy as she was, and in the same dilemma. She solved their dilemma one morning by saying "Maybe you'd like to put a name to our 'hellos.' "

Ben, a philosophy professor in his middle forties, found conversation with people he didn't know well, particularly women, difficult — until he discovered that there is nothing more rare, engaging, and flattering than a good listener. I had suggested that he relax about making a "first impression" and concentrate instead on drawing people out. I suggested such phrases as: "That sounds interesting." "Yes, go on." "Oh, tell me more."

Being as bright and witty as he was, Ben wasn't contented to be just a listener for long. But he did find that listening gave him time to relax and feel at ease, knowing that he didn't have to begin by impressing someone.

You've come some distance since you began this book — unlearning myths, anxiety, jealousy, and loosening guilty old ties. At the same time you have been learning strength — learning to see yourself in a better, more realistic light. Leaving anxieties and fears behind you makes you stronger, gives you more time and energy to develop your own values, to trust your own judgment and build confidence.

Other people, strangers and lovers, take their cues about you from you. Developing and enhancing your self-image can become your greatest strength. It is part and parcel of knowing yourself and liking yourself. Feeling good about feeling good begins with feeling good about yourself, liking the way you look, liking what you do, liking what you think and what you feel.

8

The Basics

Of all creatures great and small, Homo sapiens (you and I and everybody else) are the most elaborate lovers on earth. There are those who say that our sex is as simple as canine coupling. And no doubt sometimes, on one level, it might be. Yet there is always more. For the elderly couple climbing into their marriage bed for the many thousandth time, for two camp counselors on a blanket while the campers are sleeping, for a couple meeting secretly in a motel on the other side of town, for two international travelers spending the night in Vienna — for all of us there is more. We have all that the animals have in sex. We have the sensations of touch, warmth, and slipperiness, the sounds and smells and the rush of desire. We have that and more.

We have our sense of memory, a sense of the present and the future. We have our fantasies, hopes, tensions, hang-ups, needs, and special pleasures. We each have our own habits, quirks, themes, and variations of personality. We have a sense of what is right and what is wrong. We have that most sophisticated, sensitive means of communication, language. And we have tenderness, caring, intimacy, romance, and love.

These are the qualities that make us human. And they are there only as possibilities . . .

What I would like to do here is to spell out a straightforward guide to lovemaking — one that includes the range of human experience, goes beyond sex manuals, and gives you access to the magnificent possibilities of human sexuality.

Just for now, put aside the way you usually make love and read this chapter as if it were an outline for the next time you make love. This is not the one and only way or sequence for making love. In fact, it is only the restrictions of the printed page that force me to arrange things here in sequence. Some things you may like to try right away, some you may want to save for later, and some you may not want to try at all. Pick and choose what you like.

COURTSHIP

Birds do it. Even butterflies and bees do it. How have we come to neglect this most elegant, basic primary step in sex? Courtship is the time when you can account for, ignore, celebrate, and reconcile individual differences. It is the time to establish trust and intimacy as you begin to learn about each other intellectually, emotionally, and physically.

If you skip courtship, you risk running into anxiety and disappointment. But more to the point, why should you skip it when it's such a wonderful chance to be romantic and playful?

Courtship is the time when certain words are important. Words such as "You're good to be with," "I want to know more about you," "I love the feel of you" begin to weave people sexually together. Holding hands, looking into each other's eyes, kissing on the street and not caring if anybody's watching, having dinner in a special restaurant, dancing, talking, whispering secrets can all create a bond between you of special meanings, shared understandings, and desire. Complimenting each other and noticing the cut of her skirt, the scent of her perfume or his after-shave, the curve of her cheek, the back of his neck can help to build up a special intimacy.

Courtship can go on and on for years. Some of the corny things become wonderful — when you walk in the rain, listen to a special song, hold hands in the movies. Especially if you take the time it requires to build desire and trust, and discover what it is that creates a romantic mood for both of you. Even if you've been together for years, it's still a shame to skip sexual courtship. After all, why should you lose the days and nights of wine and roses?

NECKING

It's time we revived the old pre-pill ritual called necking. It was so sexy.

Necking, or making out, is kissing and touching, pausing and exploring. It's kissing eyes and fingertips, hands and face and mouth. It's using your tongue and lips to make patterns on your partner's neck. And touching hair and face and arms and back and fingers in different ways with your fingers. It's using your tongue behind an ear or a knee. It's kissing, kissing, and kissing.

I suppose the closest many people come to necking is characterized by the unfortunate term *foreplay* (as if the kissing, hugging, caressing, and fondling were lesser events on the way to intercourse). But necking, or making out, really doesn't have to be just a warm-up for coitus. Necking is good, sweet, and lovely. All by itself.

We live in a competitive goal-oriented society. "Profit," "promotion," "success," "touchdown" are common battle cries. When that performance mentality is brought into sex, sex and pleasure suffer. Worry about this type of move or that one, or "Will I have an orgasm?" or "Will I satisfy him/her?" interferes with and blocks pleasure. On the other hand, necking reduces performance demands. "How do I, uh, neck?" one young marketing executive asked me. "Necking is more learning than it is knowing," I told him. "It's not as if you have to know certain ways of kissing or subtle caresses. The only thing you really *need* to know in necking is how to learn, because necking doesn't have any positions or beginnings or endings. Making out is learning how to make love."

You begin with a touch or a kiss. And see how it is received and how it feels. Tentatively or boldly, you try one thing and then, perhaps, another. Necking is free-form kissing and holding and caressing. There isn't any goal or time limit other than discovering what gives you both pleasure.

By sidetracking the rush into bed, making out addresses itself to your needs for affection and all-over loving. Necking teaches you to take all the time you need. And to learn to enjoy the stray wanderings of playfulness, for who knows where they may lead?

You can discover that you have more pleasures than you realize. (Men too often numb their feelings by narrowing their focus to genitals. Women often exclude much of their sensuality by concentrating on orgasms.) Making out is a wonderful way of drawing you out, helping you discover the sensuality in your hands or feet, chest, neck, or . . .

Necking is a time when you can try silly things. The pressure's off and the stakes are low. If something doesn't work out, you can laugh about it. It is a time to experiment and explore. We are all creatures of habit. Often when a couple has been living together for a while, their lovemaking falls into a pattern. They get into bed, roll toward each other, and . . . Necking is a wonderful antidote to the dullness of habit, simply because it encourages communication and improvisation.

You may make some unique discoveries when you communicate openly with each other, when you say what pleases you and what doesn't. Communication doesn't have to be in words. A little "hummmm" or a frown or a smile or a touch can be just right. In fact, you might call necking a way of developing a private language between you and your partner — a language with touches, kisses, and caresses for its vocabulary.

Necking is also the time when you can set the mood for lovemaking with candlelight, low lights, a romantic dinner, classical or rock music. Marijuana, like rock music, is certainly not for everyone, and some people find it increases their anxiety or has no effect at all. But others report that marijuana intensifies sensation, lengthens and intensifies the male orgasm, helps some women to have an orgasm (or orgasms) more easily, and slows the pace down so that you might spend five or ten minutes enjoying a single caress. I am not recommending that you try it, but I would be less than candid if I didn't report that many people find that marijuana intensifies sexual pleasure.

UNDRESSING

Even if you've been living together for a while and even if you're going to bed together after a long, hard day, and want to take a bath to get refreshed and comfortable — even then it's sometimes nice to bathe and then get dressed again so that undressing can be part of your lovemaking.

Couples who have been together for years tend to forget how exciting it can be to feel the texture of silks and satins, shirts and trousers beneath their fingertips — the slow, erotic tease of touching a lover here and there through clothes, the arousing promise of reaching under a skirt or of touching a man's pants and feeling him rise.

There are many ways to undress. I'd just like to mention some of them. You can take off your own clothes, one at a time, slowly, while the other person watches. Or you can take off the other person's clothes slowly, or all at once, with a lot of kissing and caressing. You can ask for help in a teasing way — "unbutton just a few buttons," "just a few snaps," "now stop." In any case, don't just throw off your clothes and jump into bed. In fact, you can leave some things on for a while. It's exciting to touch and kiss over, under, and around panties. It can be a great turn-on to kiss and caress a covered erect penis. Take off just a shirt and socks or a blouse and panties, then kiss and caress some more.

TOUCHING

Touch for your own pleasure; touch your partner because it feels good to touch that part of an arm, or neck, or thigh. And touch for the sensual experience itself, feeling the silky texture of a thigh, the crisp bristle of pubic hair, or the rising of a nipple underneath your fingertips . . . discovering whether what you are touching is warm or cool, or smooth or rough. And touch to *give* pleasure.

Vary the way you touch. A common complaint among women about the way men make love is that men are too heavy-handed and rough. I suspect there's just not enough variation. Heavy, rough touching can sometimes feel very good. By varying your touch you will be able to discover if your partner likes a firm or light brushing touch on, say, the back, or the chest. Vary your touch by using your fingertips and by using your whole hand. Try to cover legs, arms, neck, shoulders, hands, feet, and face with kisses and touches. Try touching each toe and each finger. Take them one at a time and feel each one.

If you're open to touching, new, surprisingly sensual places will turn up. Your partner's back might be sensitive when you just breathe on it or lightly run your tongue down the spine or kiss softly from the base of the spine to the neck. The head and hair can be very sensual places for kissing and caressing.

These are discoveries you have to make yourself. Explore. Spend five or ten minutes sometime touching one place other than the genitals or breasts.

Touching a Woman's Breasts

Take a slow, gradual approach. Many women don't like their breasts touched before they are sexually involved and aroused. Start by touching a woman's breasts through her clothing, and then stop. Talk and kiss and hold each other. Later, if she wears a bra, take off her blouse and touch her through her bra. There are lots of good ways to caress breasts. Some are good for some women and not so good for others. Put your whole hand over her breast. Some women find that very simulating. Some find it painful. Go slowly, and go gently. Don't go right for the nipples, though. Some women never like direct nipple stimulation. Some women love it and love to be pinched on the nipple. You might try, at first, gentle, circular brushing with your fingertips around the edge of the nipple. An erect nipple may increase a woman's breast sensitivity, which may mean that more stimulation — rubbing back and forth across the nipple quite rapidly — would feel very good. Or it may mean that more would be too much.

Sometimes lubricating her nipple with your own saliva can be an exciting sensation. Having a woman lick your finger and then using that finger to stroke her nipple can be terrifically erotic. Or a turn-off. Sex is individual, complicated, which is what is so marvelous about it. Go slowly, sample and savor the sensations, testing and pausing.

Breasts can also caress as well as be caressed, give as well as receive pleasure. A woman can brush her breasts all over her lover's body, across arms, thighs, and even feet. Some men love to have their penis caressed by breasts. A woman can take one breast and rub it all over a penis. She might also rub the head of the penis against her nipple. And possibly she can cup both breasts around the penis, stroking the penis up and down. You can experiment with oil or lotion between the breasts or on the penis, so that the penis slides easily between the breasts.

Touching a Man's Chest

Spend some time running your fingertips over large areas of his chest. Some men like to be touched lightly on their chests, while others like their nipples pinched hard. Some men like to have you circle the nipple with your finger. As with women, there are no hard and fast rules, but there are a lot of possibilities. For example, you might try letting your hair drift over his whole body, brushing his chest, legs, and genitals for a very light and erotic massage.

Touching the Clitoris

The clitoris, a small, enormously sensitive, elusive, sometimes invisible organ, is difficult for some men to understand. The tiny clitoris has as many nerve endings as does the head of a penis. The nineteenth-century sexologist Havelock Ellis once remarked that most men attempting to stroke a woman's clitoris were like an orang-utan trying to play the violin.

It takes time, understanding, and communication for a woman's partner to learn to give her pleasure from her clitoris. Again, there are no rules, because there are so many variations from one woman to the next, but there are a few tentative guidelines.

If you have any doubts about where your partner's clitoris is, you may save frustration and time by asking her to guide your hand to it. Plan to spend some enjoyable time there, with a lot of variation. Be sure there is lubrication; otherwise clitoral stimulation may hurt. Lubrication can be brought from the inside of the vagina to the clitoris. Spermicidal jelly, a non-perfumed body lotion (perfume can be an irritant), baby oil, or saliva can also be used as lubricants.

Vary where you touch the clitoris, how softly or strongly, with one finger or several, rapidly or slowly. You can go around the clitoris, for example, and sometimes you might rub the clitoris directly. Some women love direct clitoral stimulation, some women don't like it at all, and some like it just a little bit at a time. Vary the speed with which you touch. As the woman gets to higher levels of excitement, she will probably want more rapid stimulation with more intense pressure. That's not always true, but it often is. Some women get aroused when you insert your finger into their vagina. Most do not.

What's tricky is that the clitoris often disappears under the clitoral hood during the plateau, or high-arousal, stage, just when a woman may desire clitoral stimulation the most. But even though the clitoris is "gone," you can continue to stimulate it indirectly. At this point, lubrication is extremely important, because the sensitivity level of the clitoris is very high.

Generally, a woman appreciates hearing some reassurance from you, that you're not feeling impatient or bored with manual stimulation. By the same token, a woman can tell her partner that he/she doesn't have to do this "unless you'd really like to." Reciprocal pleasure is very important now. You may find that her arousal turns you on. (I would guess that about half of arousal is the arousal of the other person.) Letting your partner know that touching her and arousing her is exciting for you is one very good way to let her know you're not impatient.

Teasing, touching for a little while, stopping, doing something else, then touching a little more is a fine clitoral technique. It's good for two reasons. First, it deals with clitoral sensitivity by giving that supremely sensitive organ a rest from time to time. And it heightens excitement. (Bringing your partner — male or female — to a very high peak of arousal and then stopping not only lengthens sexual play and draws out the pleasure, it also allows your partner to reach a higher, more intense peak later.)

Touching the Penis

Many men complain that women are too light-handed in touching their penis. Women say that they are afraid of hurting the man. But men and women rarely talk about these needs and fears with each other. Many women feel inadequate and uncertain about touching a man's penis. Just as a woman has to show and tell her partner how she likes to have her clitoris touched, so too must a man guide his partner through the idiosyncratic mysteries of touching his penis. I can give you some guidelines, but your best teacher is your partner.

Start slowly. Touch the penis very lightly at first. A nice place to start is on the testicles, with light, all-over fingertip touching, with, perhaps, light pinching. Some men like to have the hair on their testicles given gentle or sharp little tugs. Some men don't.

One hand is generally enough for stroking a penis. As you start from the bottom of the penis and move up the shaft, you can intensify the pressure as you get closer to the head of the penis. That's the way many men masturbate, closing their hand firmly around their penis and stroking up and down, intensifying pressure as their hand moves up.

Start stroking slowly. As his arousal increases, you can increase the speed and intensify the pressure.

Incidentally, erections come and go. They wax and they wane during making out. So neither of you should be upset if the man loses his erection. If you don't worry about it it's more likely to come back.

Lubrication, such as baby oil or the man's pre-ejaculate fluid, can be very helpful, especially around the sensitive head of the penis. If you get tired you can change hands, or you can alternate hands from time to time to vary the sensation, speed, and pressure on the penis. And as you learn your partner's excitement pattern, you can heighten his pleasure and help him to last longer by teasing: building up to a high level of excitement and stopping, building up and stopping. Many men find teasing an exciting and enhancing prelude to orgasm.

KISSING

Kissing can be more intimate than intercourse. Kissing a lover on the mouth can be erotic, intimate, and voluptuous. A kiss can be full of news, separate events, and surprises. An old Hindu saying tells us that "A long kiss is better than a short coitus." There is a lot more to kissing than the simple lip-to-lip kiss. In kissing, you can use your lips and your tongue, letting your tongue explore your partner's tongue and teeth and mouth.

You can make a special event of kissing the whole body, from the head to the toes, covering your partner with kisses. Talk between kisses. There's no need for lovemaking to be a silent affair. Don't always keep your eyes closed while you're kissing. Keeping your eyes open encourages talking and communicating with sounds, hugs, tugs, murmurs, and moans.

Try kissing hands and palms. For many women, having their hands kissed is a great turn-on, harking back to the days of swords, capes, and chivalry. One delicious variation is to suck each finger in turn. Some people become orgasmic when their toes are sucked. You might try sucking on each of your partner's toes, using your tongue and lips. You can run the point of your tongue along the back of the toes. Vary the sucking and kissing of fingers and toes — light and hard, short and long, deep and shallow — using your tongue for emphasis.

Kissing Her Breasts

Kissing the female breasts can vary tremendously in terms of what is pleasurable. Try kissing the whole breast with your lips and tongue. You can run your tongue around the edge of the nipple. Search and explore for the more sensitive parts of the nipple. Use the flat of your tongue to lick the nipple and the surrounding area as you would lick an ice-cream cone. You can flick your tongue back and forth across her nipples or suck on them gently or roughly. (According to Kinsey, eleven per cent of women have orgasms from breast stimulation. Some women hate having their breasts touched and kissed, while others feel neutral about it.) You can move from one breast to the other, and touch other places while you're kissing a breast. The woman can guide her partner's head with her hands to show where and how she wants to be kissed on her breasts. These are just a few of the possibilities. You will discover more.

Kissing His Chest

Many men love to have their chest and nipples kissed, licked, and sucked. Kissing the man's chest can be very similar to kissing a woman's breasts, but you might try more pressure, and concentrate more on the nipples using a sharp, pointed tongue or a broad, flat tongue. You can cover the whole nipple with your mouth and suck gently or roughly on the nipple and the area surrounding it. As with women, there's a wide variation. What some men like leaves other men cold.

ORAL SEX

There's a certain amount of mystery surrounding oral sex. Kissing genitals can be a very intense and pleasurable part of lovemaking. However, you may be repelled by the idea and want to skip over this section. Let me emphasize that you shouldn't do anything you don't want to do. If you feel any discomfort, stop. If you're just learning, take gradual steps, and take them slowly and tentatively.

The tongue and mouth seem to be particularly well-suited

for stimulating the vaginal lips and the clitoris. There's a lot you can do with the tongue, especially if you take your time — circular licks around the clitoris, long strokes, short ones, darting in and out of the vagina. Some of this will feel very good for some women, and not so good for others. Vary, experiment, and discover. You might try taking the clitoris very gently between your lips and sucking lightly as you stroke the tip of the clitoris with your tongue. You might also try kissing and sucking and licking the inner lips of the vagina.

Using your tongue on the clitoris directly or indirectly can be intensely pleasurable, because the tongue itself is so sensitive, supple, and wet. You can use long, hard strokes or soft, gentle strokes, or rapid flicking strokes back and forth across the clitoris with the tip of your tongue. Use the tip of your tongue to search and explore for the clitoris as it recedes under its hood during moments of high excitement. Remember, with as many nerve endings in the tiny clitoris as in the head of a penis, very short strokes in a tiny area can produce a tremendous amount of sensation.

Kissing a man's penis can be just as varied. One nice way to begin is to take the penis in your mouth before it's erect. It's an easy way to get used to a penis, since it's not nearly so big as when it's erect. And it can be extremely exciting for the man.

Like the clitoris, the head of the penis will probably be thrilled by your tongue and your lips. You don't have to take the whole penis in your mouth (the gag reflex prevents most lovers from doing so), but you can move your hand up and down the shaft to give stimulation to the rest of the penis as you take part of the penis in your mouth.

Having his penis thrust in and out of your mouth can be part of oral sex with a man, but there are many other things you might try. For example, suck on the head and upper shaft of the penis, intensifying the pressure with your lips as you approach the head. Use your lips to give him firm or light kisses along the shaft, darting your tongue in and out all over the penis. Or you can start at the base of the penis and with your tongue go back and forth on the shaft, varying the pressure on up to the head of his penis, and then use your tongue to go round and round the head and the rim. And (and this applies to both men and women) don't neglect the whole pubic area for licks and kisses. Your lover may find it very erotic to have his pubic hair tugged with your lips. And some people like little bites and pinches. Some don't.

Before and during kissing the penis you might try light kisses on the testicles, making little gentle bites of the skin with your lips. Sucking a testicle softly or quite hard can be erotic. It may be quite painful. There's a fine line between pleasure and pain. A man should teach his partner just how much pressure gives him pleasure, and how much causes pain.

Oral sex may not be a turn-on for you. I've talked to many people who felt inadequate because they just weren't aroused by taking a man's penis in their mouth. You may want to do it anyway, to give your partner pleasure. But by all means don't do it if it causes anxiety or you just don't want to. And if it doesn't excite you, don't worry about it. Lots of people don't find it exciting.

As for the man's ejaculating in your mouth, that's really a matter of your own preference. (I might point out that the average ejaculate has only sixteen calories, along with enzymes and lots of protein.) You can stop oral stimulation before ejaculation if you want to. Or you can pull away right after the ejaculation has begun, so you get only a bit of ejaculate in your mouth. If that feels O.K., you can try more, taking the penis more deeply in your mouth the next time. If the thought of taking ejaculate in your mouth repels you, don't do it. On the other hand, if you find you can think about it as an adventure, and if you want to try it, then you can do it in small, graduated steps over a period of time until you feel comfortable with it.

INTERCOURSE

Wait as long as you possibly can. Then wait some more. Whether that means for months in an ongoing affair or for later in the evening, I strongly recommend that intercourse be put off for as long as possible.

Intercourse has more symbolic meaning than most people realize. Most of us were taught that intercourse is only for marriage and making babies, that it implies a lifelong commitment.

Times have changed since those early lessons. Many people aren't waiting for marriage. There are any number of moral values and sexual possibilities. The guidelines I would suggest for intercourse are: be caring and loving, and share trust and intimacy. I think you should also feel comfortable with what you are doing and have intense erotic feelings. And I think you should both recognize and share responsibility for contraception and the consequences of your relationship. When these conditions are met, then there is a good possibility that intercourse will be wonderful.

People who are accustomed to having intercourse on a first or second date can't imagine waiting a month or six months or a year before having intercourse. And yet that is how long it might take a couple before intercourse can be a wonderful, pleasurable experience. Ideally, intercourse should also flow out of the whole process of necking and kissing and touching — and a state of arousal so high that it is inevitable and irresistible. That is in strong contrast to such common reasons as: you finally have a room to yourselves, it's your first date, it's your honeymoon, you're afraid you might lose him/her, or you're curious about what it's like. An important reason *not* to have intercourse is because you haven't discussed contraception.

Intercourse itself can be awkward, especially if you are having it together for the first time. To smooth the way, the man or the woman can take the head of the man's penis and move it around the outer lips of the vagina, around the vaginal opening, and around the clitoris. This can be highly arousing for both of you. And it might avoid the fumbling awkwardness of trying to find the entrance to the vagina. Using the penis to caress can also be an arousing way to interrupt intercourse, since it gives the woman direct clitorial stimulation and the man extra stimulation on the head of the penis.

If the woman has an orgasm before intercourse, it can help to take the pressure off both of you and allow you to enjoy intercourse instead of working at it. As we've seen, a woman is less likely to have an orgasm during intercourse than through manual or oral stimulation. (For those who would rush into intercourse as the goal of lovemaking, it's interesting to note that many women actually experience a decline in sexual pleasure with penetration.)

Many women do not get aroused from stimulation inside the vagina, which means that manual stimulation of the clitoris during intercourse is important. Manual stimulation of the man's genitals can intensify his pleasure, too. Therefore, you should try to find positions that not only are comfortable, but that also allow you to caress each other during intercourse.

There are four basic positions, with an almost infinite number of variations:

The woman-on-top position is best for the woman's being able to move around and add to her own stimulation. When she's on top, a woman has an easier time controlling the pace and intensity. She may also find that she can rub her clitoris against her partner with the precise pressure and variation that only she knows. When the woman is sitting on top, it is relatively easy for her to touch herself or for the man to touch her clitoris to increase her excitement.

The man-on-top (or "missionary") position is best when the man is nearing his orgasm. He can thrust very deeply and the extra muscle tension he gets in this position can intensify his orgasm. In addition, if the pelvises are very close and moving together, a woman can get a good deal of pelvic stimulation, particularly if, instead of thrusting in and out, the man slides up and down against her pelvis while his penis is deep inside her. One disadvantage of the man-on-top position is that it limits a woman's movements, and thereby may limit her clitoral stimulation. And unless a man supports himself on his hands and knees, his weight on the woman may be another disadvantage in this position.

The side positions face-to-face may be a little awkward. But the intimacy and the ability of either partner to move can be very nice. Side-by-side and face-to-face can be very relaxed and comfortable, because no one is carrying any weight. It's a position that makes manual stimulation easy for both partners. And it's the kind of position that makes it easy to stop for a while and just talk, kiss, or touch.

The rear-entry position, from either the side or the top, gives intense stimulation to the man, because of the very deep thrusting into the woman's vagina and the muscular massage of his penis by her thighs and buttocks. It can be fabulous for many women and terrible for others. The only clitoral stimulation a woman can obtain in this position is manual.

Feel free to stop intercourse and rest, cuddle, and talk. Stop and just kiss and touch for a while. Most people, once they start intercourse, feel compelled to continue, nonstop, to orgasm or exhaustion. But stopping is a great arouser. It also helps a man last longer. It's a time when you can be very close and intimate, and a time when, with manual stimulation, a woman might enjoy an orgasm.

Orgasm covers a multitude of happenings. Collectively, they may range in intensity from a small sigh to a typhoon of sensation. (If you'd like to know more about the physiological phenomena of your sexual responses — what happens in your body when you're making love — you'll find a detailed outline at the end of this chapter.)

Intensifying the Male Orgasm: Techniques to Use During Intercourse

Going up to and then backing away from an orgasm can increase its ultimate intensity. And it's a good technique for prolonging a man's lovemaking. There is one small catch. After delaying an orgasm several times in an evening, some men then have difficulty having an orgasm that evening.

Several other things can increase the intensity of the male orgasm. His partner can touch his testicles and squeeze them, sometimes quite roughly, or push them back against the perineum as he approaches and has an orgasm. She may be able to insert her finger in her vagina during intercourse and stimulate his penis there. Or she can caress his pelvis or pull slightly on his pubic hair or squeeze his nipples. Generally, the "missionary position" is the best for these manual variations.

A man might increase the intensity of his orgasm by tensing his thigh muscles prior to orgasm, thrusting deeper, and increasing the speed of his thrusting.

Both men and women are often very sensitive to anal stimulation: rubbing the anus with your finger or very gently inserting your finger in your partner's anus. If you feel comfortable about anal stimulation, which is not for everyone, you might find that it adds to the intensity of intercourse and orgasm — especially if you do it just before an orgasm.

Intensifying the Female Orgasm: Techniques to Use During Intercourse

The question I'm asked most often by women who come to see me in therapy and by women in the audiences of seminars is "How can I have an orgasm during intercourse?"

There are several ways to heighten pleasure during intercourse that may lead to the woman's orgasm. It's an excellent idea, for example, to wait until the woman is just about to have an orgasm before penetration, and then continue manual stimulation during intercourse.

The bottom (the back) of the vaginal opening is, for some women, tremendously sensitive to being rubbed against by the base of the penis. In other words, along with the in-and-out strokes a man might try some up-and-down strokes, so that the base of his penis stimulates the bottom of the mouth of the vagina.

An excellent exercise to intensify the pleasure of intercourse is a vaginal-muscle contraction suggested by Dr. Arnold Kegel, an obstetrician in California. The muscle that stops and starts the flow of urine is also the muscle that contracts during orgasm. If you can make that muscle stronger you'll probably be more likely to have an intense orgasm. You can begin to practice contracting that muscle during urination, with your knees about one foot apart. After you have located the muscle in this way, simply contract and relax it at will ten times before you get out of bed in the morning, ten times each time you sit down to eat, and so on. Notice and focus on the sensations inside your vagina as you contract the muscle. Work up to a hundred contractions a day. (This exercise, which strengthens and makes you aware of the muscle that contracts in rapid waves during orgasm, can be a wonderful turn-on all by itself. One woman, who has become adept at the exercise — which can be done any time, anywhere — says, "Nobody on the bus knows why I'm smiling.") Next, contract and relax the muscle as you masturbate, or during clitoral and vaginal stimulation. You might try inserting your finger into your vagina and contracting around your finger rapidly, and also quite slowly. You might then try doing these muscle contractions around your partner's penis during a slow or still moment in intercourse. This can feel wonderful for both of you. As one man says, "It's the most intimate hug."

Circular pelvic movement and up-and-down movements during intercourse can contribute to the intensity of your orgasm. Some women do not experience an orgasm if they don't move their pelvises. And some women prefer to be on top, so that they can better control their pelvic movement and stimulation.

Making noise can release tension and let you let yourself go. Shout, yowl, moan, and sigh if you feel like doing so.

Tensing your thigh muscles just before orgasm can produce a small increase in the strength of your orgasm.

You can experiment with different intercourse positions until you find the one or more that are conducive to the type of stimulation (direct or indirect) that you find most arousing.

Fantasies can be helpful. Let your mind have a good romantic and sexual time, too.

Some women find vibrators helpful or even necessary for stimulation to orgasm during intercourse.

You can't will an orgasm. And setting up an orgasm as a goal — something you are working toward — interferes with your pleasure. Don't put yourself or let your partner put you under that kind of pressure. Instead of trying to have an orgasm, focus on specific sensations, on what some of those millions of sensitive nerve endings in your hands, genitals, back, stomach, feet, and face are telling you.

An orgasm during intercourse is not a "vaginal" orgasm. An orgasm is an all-over body response to a high level of pleasure. Where that pleasure comes from — from your hands or feet or vagina or breasts or clitoris — does not define the "kind" of orgasm you have. Orgasms differ in sensation, intensity, and duration. But to call one orgasm a "clitoral" or "vaginal" orgasm is misleading — misleading because it confuses one particular area of sensation with an all-over body response.

GLOW

Many couples find it's very pleasant to stay together after ejaculation, with the man's penis remaining inside his partner.

If the woman can do some vaginal contractions around his penis, she can add to the pleasure of both. Also, a woman might still feel sexual, so it may be a good idea to continue to kiss and touch for a while.

After an orgasm there's the most intimate time of all. There's a glorious relaxing of inhibitions. Things can be talked about that just can't be discussed in another time or place. It's the perfect time to discuss what has just happened. I don't mean asking "Did you come?," but saying thinks like "I felt so shy when you . . ." or "I would like to —— next time." Talking about the whole experience, what you'd like to do more or less of, adds to the depth of the experience and the intimacy between you. It's also a time you can laugh together over the funny, awkward moments. Even if you are sleepy, you can still stay in each other's arms and enjoy the embers of sensuality. What is most important now is the intimacy. You have been on an eventful journey together and now you are in each others' arms. It can be simply beautiful.

ADDENDUM

Here, in an extended footnote, is a brief calendar of physiological events during lovemaking. It's an incomplete picture at best, leaving out the great emotions, sights, sounds, smells, textures, shapes, and romance. On the other hand, it is useful to have an accurate picture of the physical phenomena.

Arousal

You begin to feel attracted and excited, and being touched and touching turns you on. You feel desire, a compelling need to be close and physically involved. You begin to breathe faster. Your pulse rate rises. Blood rushes into your genitals faster than it goes out, so the penis becomes erect and the clitoris enlarges. (Clitoral enlargement varies; it may be hardly noticeable.) You may perspire and become flushed, and your muscles may tense as you feel increasingly excited. The sexual organs become unusually sensitive to touch. Testicles rise toward the body as the scrotal skin becomes tense and thick. The interior of the vagina begins to turn a darker pink and lubricate with a pearly fluid as the uterus begins to lift off the floor of the vaginal barrel. As excitement increases, the interior two-thirds of the vagina goes through waves of expansion and relaxation, becoming larger. The penis becomes more sensitive, with the tip becoming extremely sensitive. The inner lips of the vagina swell and deepen in color to a rich, rosy plum. The female breasts enlarge as much as twenty-five per cent, and nipples become erect and sensitive. The penis may emit a clear liquid as a lubricant. (This liquid usually contains a small amount of sperm, which means that withdrawal before orgasm is no guarantee of contraception.)

Breathing and pulse rates continue to increase. Blood pressure rises. Muscle tension becomes stronger and stronger. Women may show a blotchy measleslike (maculopapular) flush over the legs, thighs, and pelvic area. Lying on your back, you may experience carpopedal spasms (both men and women), which means your toes curl up. The inner two-thirds of the vagina continues to enlarge and become smoother, but the outer third becomes smaller and tighter, increasing the sensation between a thrusting penis and the outer vagina. The clitoris retracts under the clitoral hood. In intercourse, the thrusting of the penis pulls the inner lips of the vagina, which in turn pull the clitoral hood over the clitoris: it's this back-and-forth movement of the clitoral hood over the clitoris that produces a great part of the female stimulation during intercourse. Lubrication from the vaginal walls and from the penis continues and even increases. Just before orgasm the smaller lips of the vagina turn bright pink or a deeper rosy red. Muscle tension builds and builds.

Orgasm

In orgasm a great many things happen in such quick succession that it seems as if it's all happening at once. Blood pressure, pulse rate, and breathing rate all reach a peak. The reddish sex flush on the skin (twenty-five per cent of men and most women have it) is at its highest point. Your hands may clench and grasp. The muscles in your arms, legs, feet, and neck contract in a spasm. In a man's body, liquid from several different glands begins to flow into and collect in a bulb in the prostate gland. The fluid, collectively, is called semen. And it is at this point (the point of "inevitability"), as the semen builds up pressure, that a man knows he is going to ejaculate. Within one to five seconds after the seminal fluids have gathered in the prostatic bulb, muscles at the base of the penis contract, in three to four successive waves occurring four-fifths of a second apart, and propel the seminal fluid through the penis and out in a rush accompanied by an intense, sometimes almost unbearable, excitement, pleasure, and release. In a woman the outer third of the vagina contracts in a succession of rhythmic waves at intervals of four-fifths of a second, faster than she could contract those muscles voluntarily. The uterus also contracts rhythmically. She has three to twelve (often imperceptible) contractions, accompanied by many different feelings of intensity, pleasure, and euphoria originating in the clitoral and vaginal area and often flowing through the whole body. Both men and women may experience muscular jerking, arching, groaning, grasping, shouting, grimacing, and writhing.

Glow

In men, orgasm is followed by an almost immediate release of muscular tension and an abrupt draining of blood out of the penis and pelvic region. The penis returns to its usual size and the man is usually relaxed, and often sleepy. In contrast, a woman comes down very gradually. Some women, with varying kinds of stimulation, can go on from orgasm to orgasm, feeling more or feeling less pleasure with each successive orgasm. In any case, physiologically a woman usually experiences a much longer afterglow, a lingering feeling of warmth and pleasure. Men, on the other hand, enter another phase, called the refractory period, in which another orgasm cannot happen. An erection may or may not appear during this phase (which lasts anywhere from a few minutes to hours or days), but an orgasm is simply not physically possible.

9

Laughter in the Bedroom

There is an aphrodisiac.

And I'm happy to report that it is easier to find than rhinoceros horn, powdered Spanish insects, or panther milk.

I was asked once on a TV show if there were just one thing and only one that I could recommend to improve sex, what would it be? "Laughter," I said, "laughter in the bedroom."

Once upon a time in the bedroom, sex was shrouded in shame, anxiety, and superstition. Now that there has been a sexual revolution, celebrating performance and orgasm, sex is still, for many couples, a silent and serious ceremony.

Ah, but there is great strength in humor and joyous release in laughter. A sense of humor in bed is the world's best sexual tonic. Of course, there has been a lot of laughter *about* sex (the dirty jokes, the snickers and the sneers) but there could be much more honest, playful laughter *in* sex. Most sexual activity now takes place in silence. It's no wonder people can't laugh during sex: they can't even talk. As one woman put it, "It's hard to laugh in silence."

Sex isn't always skyrockets at night and the earth moving. You simply can't always be transported to new levels of experience. There is a lot in sex that is silly or unexpected or awkward. Laughter gives you safe and happy passage through the less than perfect moments that, given the frailty of being human, make up most of our sexual encounters.

A sense of humor in bed is the easiest and most wonderful sexual technique to experience. It's also the most difficult to describe. At its best, humor in lovemaking is intimate, gentle, and loving. Most of the humor will come out of your own experience and be your own. Humor is, after all, a matter of taste and circumstance. Memorizing a series of catchy lines for awkward moments is about as useful as storing fresh eggs in the cellar in case there's ever a shortage of fresh eggs. So I can't give you all-purpose jokes and witticisms. But I can give you some examples and guidelines.

First of all, what I'm talking about is a humorous perspective, a sense of humor — a sense that the miraculous and the ridiculous are very closely related.

Humor breaks the ice. Humor inhibits anxiety just the way relaxation and erotic feelings inhibit anxiety. Silence, on the other hand, breeds anxiety. Not saying anything when you are worried about the way you look without your clothes on can increase your anxiety. It's not necessary to be witty or especially funny ("There's a draft in here. I think I'll keep my pants on"). You might simply say you feel embarrassed. It's just that humor can be a light and gentle way of communicating.

Humor adds to intimacy, because with humor there are so many more things you can talk about. Subjects that could be barriers because they seem too embarrassing can become shared secret bridges between you. An extreme example was a woman who, after some long silences and evasive answers to my questions, finally told me that her problem was a ticklish clitoris. "I know it sounds funny, but it's terrible. I just can't bear to be touched there for fear I'm going to break out laughing, which would be a terrible blow to my husband's ego." As she was soon to discover, it wasn't a terrible problem at all. I suggested that instead of struggling and fighting against the laughter, to laugh and enjoy it. When she told her husband "Tom, I have a confession to make. It doesn't hurt when you touch my clitoris, it tickles," they both laughed. Now, instead of feeling embarrassed or confused, they have the pleasure of sharing a wonderful and sometimes hilarious secret.

A much more common anxiety would be simply feeling shy — shy about being with someone new or shy about being passionate or shy about beginning sex. We are all shy in some ways. You have many private places, many guarded emotions. Talking ("I'm wondering if you are feeling some of the same things I'm feeling") and laughing ("I have this crazy desire to see you with your socks off") can reduce your shyness. Laughing and talking go hand in hand. One leads to the other as you gain the courage to let your own foibles out into the open, not as confessions of failure or admissions of guilt, but as sharing experiences as you become intimate. Saying you're shy is really one way of conveying your trust to someone, because you are saying you are vulnerable. And there are many ways to say you're shy: "I wish I had Linus's blanket to hold on to," or "Could we do this in separate rooms?"

Awkwardness is akin to shyness, and a sense of humor can help here as well. Heaven knows, sex is full of awkward moments. Magazine advertisements encourage women to be seductive. Toothpastes, perfumes, lipsticks, lingerie, and costume jewelry all make their claim to being essential props. Marlboro men and "playboys" are supposed to have an easy time bedding whomever they wish. But the role of seducer, with either a new person or a partner of fifteen years, may be a hard one to play. Done seriously, seduction might just succeed. But you might as well recognize that while there is a lot of pleasure in seduction, there is also a lot of silliness. The big-time vamps (Mata Hari, Marlene Dietrich, Marilyn Monroe, with her bruised, innocent sensuality) seem almost like cartoon characters now — their exaggerated gestures relics from another time. And if you are prepared to laugh or smile at the situation ("Hmmm. That's not working. Maybe you'd like some chocolate ice cream") you'll probably be more seductive.

If there's something you don't want to do — kiss, neck, make love, swallow ejaculate ("I'm on a very strict diet") — humor allows you a more graceful escape route than grimly shaking your head no. I don't mean that one should feel embarrassed or reluctant to say no. Often "no" needs to be said very directly. Yet humor can give you a softer alternative.

There are so many awkward moments that humor can dispel. Perhaps no mystery more deep or profound faces Western man than how to unhook a bra, one-handed in the dark. A man in that quandary might say, "Hold still. This may take a month."

Saying almost anything is better than staying silent. If you walk in to dinner and there are candles, wine, and soft music and you feel that you are being set up, you might, instead of worrying about it and feeling tense, say something like "I think I'll skip dessert."

Humor keeps you from falling into patterns of failure. If, say, an intercourse position doesn't work, instead of feeling defeated, you can laugh about it together as an experience you shared, instead of one that drives you apart.

Both humor and anxiety are contagious. Those events that might otherwise seem momentarily tragic are, when sprinkled with humor, really opportunities to become closer — closer in the knowledge that nothing always works perfectly. Ejaculations often happen before you expect them. If premature ejaculation occurs once in a while, it would ease the tension if you could both laugh about it. The man might say "I guess you really excite me," or the woman, in a close and trusting relationship, might say "Was it something I said?"

A man, entering the refractory phase after coitus, is prone to go to sleep. A kind and humorous word from him can mean a great deal: 'You've made me very happy. And very sleepy."

For other seemingly disappointing moments (no erection, no orgasm), a kind, light word to yourself can be both realistic and reassuring. For you can use humor with yourself as well as with your partner: "It's hard for me to have an orgasm on Tuesdays."

One very common awkward moment — or rather series of awkward moments — arises from a woman's concern that she is taking a very long time to reach a high level of excitement and orgasm. A good way to defuse that anxiety is to be perfectly straightforward and say that it takes you a long time. Another way would be to use humor: "I always take ages. Would you like a book to read?"

Laughter prolongs lovemaking, takes the focus off coitus, and increases the "play" in foreplay. This is important when the woman needs an extended time for high arousal, and when the man needs to learn to slow down. Teasing, done with humor, can be a kind and caring way to slow things down while still keeping the excitement rising.

Humor is also a good way to deal with unexpected interruptions, such as the phone ringing at the worst possible time: "This must be what they mean by coitus interruptus."

Laughter can help you be a little more adventurous. If you take a new fantasy too seriously, you have no place to go if it doesn't work out, except, perhaps, into performance anxiety. On the other hand, if you are both willing to laugh, you can risk more. Laughter is a natural escape hatch that lets you be yourself, even while you run the risk of being foolish.

As for your own idiosyncrasies, laughter lets them come out, safely, into the open. Instead of your foibles being things to suppress and worry about, they can be part of the adventure, part of the shared discoveries. "You're wearing socks to bed?" "Well, I don't want to get cold feet at the last moment."

And after intense lovemaking, humor can keep the intimacy warm and shared, avoiding the embarrassment you might feel after making all that noise: "We could have been arrested for disturbing the peace."

For honeymooners, laughter can be part of the trousseau. After all, there's so much pressure and ceremony attached to the honeymoon night, the one night when you are most apt to be totally exhausted and just want to go to sleep. Laughter can help you do just that. Laugh at the irony that now lovemaking is legal and you can do it with the world's blessing, and all you want to do is sleep.

Most of what I have reported here has been verbal humor, because that's by far the easiest to communicate on a page. But there is a whole other, nonverbal vocabulary — bites, tickles, grunts, pokes, teases, touches, kisses, and licks — that can be at least as articulate in expressing the sense of humor that can almost always be present in this awkward, improbable juxtaposition of two people.

Finally, let me emphasize once again that what counts is not the humor itself — whether you have a snappy delivery or a clever line — but the *sense* of humor: that sex is enormously complex, elaborate, and rarely perfect, but often funny.

A sense of humor is a pleasure and a tonic all on its own. For love may make the world go round, but it's laughter that makes love go round.

10

Everybody Has a Problem Sometimes

LEARNING TO OVERCOME
SEXUAL DYSFUNCTION

In all the magic and music of sex, there's a certain sloppiness. Nature, in its constant changes, sometimes takes unexpected, even malicious turns. Just when everything is going right — something goes wrong. A penis, however coaxed and cuddled, refuses to stand up. A hoped-for orgasm runs away and hides. A man ejaculates too soon.

People rarely discuss their sexual problems. It's as if an unachieved orgasm or an unerect penis were a sign of weakness, of a poor relationship, a bad lover, an unmanly man, or an unwomanly woman. The deep silence surrounding sexual problems leads one to believe that nobody else has this happen to them, that everyone else's sex is perfectly trouble-free and unpunctuated by these physical letdowns. For many years the old Hollywood movie camera coyly averted its lens to the ripples on the pond just as sex was beginning (Buddy Hackett once said, "For years I thought foreplay led to drowning"). And since sex among consenting adults was assumed to be perfectly beautiful, anything less than that was unmentionable.

Even now, there's little understanding of the common sexual dysfunctions.

Sexual dysfunction is a subject I teach to gynecologists, urologists, psychiatrists, and medical students. Even they turn tightlipped and stony-faced when it comes to discussing their own sexual dysfunctions. And many of them flinch when their patients begin discussing sexual problems.

It is crucial to understand the symptoms, causes, cures, and prevention of sexual dysfunction, because you will experience some sexual problems at least some of the time. Sexual dysfunction is at least as common as the common cold. And in most cases it's less serious, particularly if you know how to deal with the problem and deal with it right away.

My associate Dr. William K. Kirby and I have had virtually a hundred per-cent success in curing erection problems among college males. Granted, part of the reason is their youth; they don't have years of repetition and reinforcement that can make a sexual problem more difficult to cure. But most important, college students are now willing to come in and deal with a problem that happened the night before — a problem that their parents might have suffered in silence for twenty years.

In looking for causes, it's easy to assume that sexual problems are the result of a flaw in the relationship. But there's rarely any straightforward equation between a good/bad relationship and good/bad sex. Bad sex does not necessarily mean that something is wrong with the relationship. I've seen numerous couples who have a beautiful, close, caring relationship and unhappy sex. And vice versa.

It's true, sexual problems can arise from problems in a relationship, but they can also come from specific anxieties, faulty techniques, or your upbringing. No one, as I've said, is immune. Everybody has a problem sometime. If you summarize life in terms of sexuality, some common problems emerge in a pattern.

SEXUAL PASSAGES

Late Adolescence. A time of awkwardness and fumbling, which can be very beautiful if it's a shared adventure. But it's common for a young woman to find no enjoyment in sex, because: (a) she believes sex is wrong and dirty; (b) she believes in the ancient Chinese method of contraception — lie still and as long as you don't enjoy it, you won't get pregnant; (c) she has not learned how to have an orgasm; (d) she is doing it to "keep the guy," or because "everybody else is." Young men have erection problems, because it's their first time and they are scared and don't know what to do. They have premature-ejaculation problems, because they've been conditioned by hurried, furtive masturbation and because they are young and inexperienced.

Young Singles (Early Twenties). For many women now, having sex is easy, but becoming aroused and having an orgasm is not. They find that they are feeling guilty and anxious about sex, because it means "breaking Mom and Dad's rules." There's a lot of nonintimate sex, as young "lovers" skip the major part of sexuality and go straight to coitus. Some men, trying to live up to a "stud" image, have erection problems, because you can't always, any time, anyplace, have an erection. Also, they often find that heavy drinking interferes with their erections.

And at this age, as in late adolescence, young men are prone to feeling guilty and anxious about homosexual feelings.

Marriage (Midtwenties and Thirties). Nobody talks about the sexual problems they had on their honeymoon. As a result, you tend to feel you are the only one who had a disaster in place of perfect bliss.

After a new baby, a woman may feel some depression, which blocks sexual arousal. She may also feel physical pain with intercourse, especially when she and her partner rush back into intercourse rather than taking their time.

The "seven-year itch" may arrive, when sex ceases to hold any surprises or adventures, when sex may become "rutting" — a boring, automatic ritual. As pleasure disappears, sexual problems flourish. Not the least of these is the loss of physical attraction for each other and the search for sexual pleasure elsewhere.

Alcohol begins to take its toll now, as some men find erection problems increasing along with their drinking.

Middle Age (Forties and Fifties). This is a hard time for men, when they ask difficult questions about their whole lives, including their sexuality. They worry about their sexual ability as they find they need more direct stimulation to get an erection and as they find their refractory period extending, so that they can't have sex quite so frequently. If they've had a sexual problem before, it may become more entrenched now.

Women tend to be just as worried about aging. Particularly at menopause, they worry about losing their sexual desire and desirability. They fear that menopause means that their sex life is over.

Sixties and Beyond. The myth that sex is for the young takes a heavy toll. For example, some fifty per cent of men at age seventy-five have erection problems because the myth becomes a self-fulfilling prophecy. People get scared with the changes in aging (it now takes longer to get an erection and women may find they have less lubrication), because these changes are unexpected and assumed to signal the end of their sexual life.

*

There are varying degrees of each of these problems, ranging from severe, long-term problems to occasional, mild difficulties. Problems that are mild and of recent origin I believe I can help you deal with in these pages. If you have had a specific problem for years, you will probably find this chapter helpful, but you will also probably need more extensive advice and assistance. (I should also point out that vaginismus, in which the vagina contracts in spasm to prevent intercourse, and dyspareunia, painful intercourse, are best treated by a specialist and are outside the scope of this chapter. The problem of no orgasm in women is also outside the scope of this chapter. I apologize for treating three male problems to just one female problem in the pages that follow. I'm not biased. It's just that there are more male sexual problems that lend themselves to specific, short-term programs.) If you have a chronic problem, you should seek help, because most sexual problems are amenable to treatment.

Now let's look at the four most common sexual problems, their causes, cures, and preventions.

THE MOST COMMON SEXUAL PROBLEMS

Erection Problems

Every man doesn't have an erection sometime. Some men never have an erection. Most men have a problem with an erection from time to time. Some men can have an erection only with a certain person or certain kind of person (their wife, a lover, a prostitute), but not with another kind of person (their wife, a lover, a prostitute).

Erections are so important to men but so rarely discussed that the subject is riddled with misconceptions. One man took a month off from his work and traveled a thousand miles to have his "impotence" treated. "What," I asked him, "do *you* mean by 'impotence'?" He told me that he was having sex about seven times every two days and about once in those seven times he has no erection. I told him to go home and rest. "That's not 'impotence,' that's just the limits of human endurance."

It's easy to joke about erection difficulties if they are somebody else's. But it's not at all funny if you have them. The major cause of erection problems is anxiety, often performance anxiety: "Am I a good lover?" "Is my penis big enough?" "Will I have an erection?" Any of those questions leads to your becoming an anxious, distant observer of your own sexual performance. "How hard is my erection?" "How long will it last?" "Is it as good as other men's?" That kind of thinking can easily inhibit erections. And the lack of an erection can produce more performance anxiety — a self-defeating, vicious circle that can get worse and worse.

Other causes of erection problems are: depression, alcoholism, an unresponsive partner (particularly for loving, sensitive men), anxiety about fantasies, anxiety about a first experience with a new partner, anger, not liking the person you're in bed with, homosexual anxiety, boredom, fatigue, general tension, a bad mood.

Aside from alcohol and alcoholism, the chances of non-erection's having a physiological cause are slight, about two per cent, but still the possibility of physiological causes should be checked by a urologist. It is possible that erection difficulties are the result of untreated diabetes, diabetic neuropathy, radical prostatic surgery (a rare kind of prostate surgery), certain hypertensive medications (prescribed for high blood pressure), large doses of some antidepressant drugs, or some endocrinological disorders, such as a low testosterone level. If you are noticing a gradually increasing random difficulty with erections, or if you are no longer having morning erections regularly, I strongly suggest that you see a urologist. (Particularly if you have a family history of diabetes.)

Prevention, of course, is the best cure, and there are many ways to prevent erection problems:

1. Don't make love when you're exhausted.
2. Don't have more than one or two drinks before sex.
3. Don't make love when you're tense.

4. Introduce as much variety into your lovemaking as possible. (Something I'll deal with in chapter 12, "A Sensual Holiday.")

5. Focus on pleasure instead of performance.

6. Instead of sex being "a deadly serious business," as one troubled executive put it, make it a romp, a playful encounter.

7. It's helpful to know that you will need more direct stimulation as you get older. A man of twenty-eight needs more stimulation than a man of twenty-two. A man of seventy-eight will need considerably more.

All of these things will help prevent erection problems, but you must realize that there will still be times when you don't have an erection. It's just part of being male.

First Aid for Occasional or Very Recent Erection Problems:

1. Ban intercourse and erections. As soon as you notice the beginning of an erection, tell your erection to go away, that it is not wanted or needed. A ban can be especially helpful if you are worried about your sexual performance. And it is often a key to the "rediscovery" of sensuality by men who have gotten into the habit of thinking of sex as just intercourse. Banning intercourse and erections takes the pressure off the man to perform. In fact, ban anything that causes you anxiety. Then gradually go back to doing it using direct calming.

2. Do other things instead of intercourse. This is a marvelous time to learn more about using your hands and your mouth — your partner is very often more responsive to your hands and your mouth than to a thrusting erect penis. (It may also be a time to learn what a pleasure it is to have your partner play with a soft penis with hands or mouth.)

3. Use direct calming. Keep to the rule of pleasure's outweighing anxiety — of never doing anything sexually that

causes you more anxiety than pleasure. Instead of worrying about whether your penis will be erect or not, concentrate on the sensations beneath your fingertips, and the sensations of your lips and tongue in kissing. As you've learned, it's not enough to try to stop thinking about something — you need another pleasurable thought, or an erotic feeling, to inhibit anxiety. You can focus on giving pleasure, or on feeling pleasure.

4. Ban alcohol. At least limit yourself to one drink or one or two glasses of wine. But if you are having occasional erection problems, it might be a good idea to ban alcohol entirely when you anticipate sexual activity.

5. Take a Sensual Holiday (see chapter 12).

6. Laugh. Laugh if you possibly can. It's a wonderful, refreshing analgesic for sexual difficulties. And laughter can be an aphrodisiac.

7. You may need more intimacy in the relationship. You may need to take more time to know and care about someone. Or you may need to find a warmer and more caring relationship.

8. When an erection disappears it can seem like a terrible loss. For some men, it seems as if their virility, their male existence, is at least suspect and maybe even a sham. That's not true, of course, but truth has very little to do with these feelings and the emotional pain can be very real and very deep. In such a case you may also need to rebuild your self-confidence. Laughter and an understanding partner can help. Beyond that, there is an excellent series of exercises called "positive image building," which you can find in my previous book, *How to Fall Out of Love*.

9. You can take direct action with graduated calming (described in chapter 5). The point is to lower your anxiety about failure, for anxiety about failure ensures failure. And if you can learn to be relaxed about not having an erection or losing an erection, you are far less likely to have the problem in the

first place. This technique then becomes part of the prevention as well as the cure.

Let me give you an example of a hierarchy you might use for dispelling erection anxieties. You recall how graduated calming works. In a state of deep muscle relaxation, you imagine the lowest item on your hierarchy for a few seconds and then go back to deep muscle relaxation. Going slowly and gradually, you repeat this process until you feel no anxiety.

NONERECTION HIERARCHY

10   Two days before a date, thinking about having no erection.

25   Making out on the sofa, you have no erection.

30   Your partner is aroused. You have no erection.

45   Your genitals being caressed through your clothes. No erection.

50   Moving into the bedroom. No erection.

55   Undressing. No erection.

60   Direct genital stimulation. No erection.

70   Oral stimulation. No erection.

80   About to penetrate and losing an erection.

90   Penetrating and then immediately losing an erection.

100   The thought "I'm never going to have an erection again."

Female Orgasm Difficulties

Now the pressure is on women to have not just one, but a whole series of orgasms. And the new criteria demand that you have one while your partner is having his.

The female orgasm can be elusive. It can be derailed by a stray worry, a voice in a distant room, a childhood memory coming out of nowhere, and, most commonly, from feeling pressure to have an orgasm. I don't mean it's as elusive as mist on a summer morning. Simply that striving for an orgasm leads to disappointment, not orgasms.

Orgasms are learned. In other words, women who have *never* had an orgasm are not shortchanged by nature, or unemotional, or unfeminine. They are *pre*-orgasmic. They have not yet learned how to have an orgasm. (Before I go any further, let me recommend an excellent book for pre-orgasmic women: *For Yourself*, by Lonnie Barbach.)

Apart from never having had an orgasm, a whole range of orgasm difficulties can occur. Some women no longer have them, although they once did. Others can have them with one partner but not another, or can have them masturbating but not with a partner. Some women have an aversion to the whole idea of sex. Some just don't seem to become aroused. Some reach very high levels of arousal but never quite reach an orgasm.

For all of these difficulties and several more besides, there is a correspondingly complex range of causes.

Some women never learned how to have an orgasm because they never learned how to masturbate. Some women don't get the right kind of stimulation from their partners. Some women have anxiety that blocks orgasms. There has always been a surfeit of feminine anxiety about sex (sex is dirty, penis fears, fear of pregnancy, and so on), and now there is the new performance anxiety I've just mentioned, a "modern woman's duty" to have multiple and simultaneous orgasms and to give her partner pleasure at the same time. Depression, anxiety, guilt about pleasure, pain, fatigue, boredom, anger, dislike of your partner, and fear of being vulnerable are all inhibitors of female orgasms.

Of course, you probably won't have an orgasm every time you have sex. But if you have had recent difficulties with orgasms, or if you used to have orgasms with reasonable frequency, but now don't, there are several things you can do.

Aids to Orgasm

1. Place a ban on anything that makes you uncomfortable in sex. Just don't do it. Follow the cardinal rule in behavior therapy, that pleasure should always outweigh anxiety.

2. Teach your partner how you want to be stimulated before and during intercourse. Tell your partner exactly how, and guide your partner's hand. (If this is difficult for you, if you are scared to do this, use a graduated approach; see chapter 11.) Some women find that self-stimulation before and during intercourse is especially effective.

3. Use a spermicidal jelly for more lubrication and to enhance sensation.

4. Take a Sensual Holiday (see chapter 12).

5. Use some pre-lovemaking turn-ons: a warm bath, sexy books, fantasizing, or masturbating, so that you are aroused when you begin lovemaking with your partner.

6. Focus on the actual sensations that you feel. Focus on what you feel in your toes and your shoulders, for example. Focus on what you feel in your genitals. Also, focus on what you feel under your fingertips as you touch your partner. And focus on giving pleasure.

7. Ask for something new, a new position, a new caress, a new place to make love.

8. You might try playing a more seductive role. The assertiveness in seduction is an aid to pleasure and to overcoming anxiety.

9. If you are observing yourself, keeping track of how near or far you feel from orgasm, then you should ban orgasms for a while. You can also ban arousal if you are worrying about becoming aroused. Without the pressure to have an orgasm or become aroused, it is likely that gradually you will experience greater pleasure.

10. If you have been faking orgasms, stop. Pretending keeps you from focusing on what you are actually feeling and leads you away from feeling aroused.

The point of all of the above is to increase your own pleasure. An orgasm is an automatic reaction to a very high level of pleasure. You cannot *will* an orgasm any more than you can will a sneeze. If there is enough pepper under your nose, you will sneeze; if there is enough pleasure in your body, you will have an orgasm. So don't work for an orgasm; that's self-defeating. But do learn to enjoy and cultivate pleasure.

Premature Ejaculation

In contrast to erection difficulties, premature ejaculation is caused not by anxiety but by physical habits that were learned in adolescence. By far the most common cause is hurried masturbation (usually due to guilt or fear of being discovered). The body simply becomes conditioned to having an orgasm very quickly. There are other less common causes that put a premium on rapid ejaculation, such as repeated experiences with prostitutes for whom time is money, or hurried, guilty sex in adolescence on the parents' living-room floor or in the back seat of a car. It can also be caused by a very high state of excitement, especially if it's the first time with a new partner. Anxiety may be a result of premature ejaculation, anxiety about your own "performance" (which can eventually cause erection problems). But that anxiety tends to retreat as you gain confidence in your ability to "last longer."

I suppose you could say that any ejaculation is premature if it happens before you or your partner want it to. But clinically we don't call an ejaculation premature unless it occurs before penetration or immediately thereafter. Kinsey's figures show that most men ejaculate within about two minutes of rapid thrusting after entering the vagina. The lesson of these figures is that it is very common to ejaculate quickly. In fact, most animals ejaculate in about four to five seconds after penetration (except for the mink, which goes on for four to five hours).

The real point, though, is that if you want to learn to take more time, you can. You can also become more versatile in giving pleasure — using your hands and mouth so that you don't have to depend solely on intercourse to give your partner pleasure.

Giving More Pleasure and Stretching the Time to Male Orgasm

1. Find other ways besides intercourse, with your hands or mouth, to help your partner to reach an orgasm before or after you have your orgasm.

2. Take as much time as necessary to help a woman reach a very high state of arousal *before* intercourse.

3. Manual stimulation of the woman during intercourse often shortens her time to orgasm, or at least increases her pleasure.

4. Do it again, if you can, after a rest. You will last longer the second time around.

5. Dr. James Semans has developed an excellent exercise for learning to delay ejaculation. You'll find it at the end of this chapter.

6. If you ejaculate before you penetrate with a new partner or if it's the *very* first time: Relax. Laugh about it. There will be other times. And that's what often happens the first time.

Delayed Male Orgasm

Occasionally, a man goes on and on but never quite reaches orgasm. When that happens regularly, the causes are most apt to be found in his early masturbation habits. Forbidden by his religion or parents to touch himself sexually, he may have rubbed against sheets or a blanket; that sensation just isn't found in intercourse. Or he may have masturbated with a very firm grip, a sensation that is also not found in intercourse. It may also be that he was, or is, a very slow, relaxed masturbator, and that it simply takes him longer than others to reach orgasm. (That can be very pleasurable for his partner.)

The time to orgasm can be shortened with the guidance of a behavior therapist. Since the treatment of chronic delayed ejaculation is complex and not within the scope of this book, I'll limit my discussion here to the far more common occasional delayed ejaculation, to the man who sometimes, because of fatigue or recent sex or both, takes a very long time and/or just can't ejaculate on that particular evening (or morning):

1. Go to sleep. Well, why not? There will be other nights and other days. And nobody can always have an orgasm.

2. Teach your partner how to masturbate you.

3. You can masturbate yourself as you stay very close to your partner. You might try entry at the very last moment.

4. You can ask your partner to stimulate you during intercourse by stroking your pelvis or testicles or the base of your penis. Or by pushing your testicles back against your perineum.

5. You can ask your partner to give you manual and/or oral stimulation during a rest period.

6. Rest for a while. Instead of continuing to try, you might find that a rest will break the pattern of "not getting anywhere."

*

Sexual problems come and go with the changes of time and seasons. Knowing that you will have them and that your partner will have them, and knowing how to deal with them adds to the romance of sexuality as well as to your self-confidence. When they do come up — and they will — you won't see them as signs of failure or symptoms of faults in your relationship. You will see them as opportunities for being closer, more understanding. You will see the inevitable changes not as losses, but as new times to learn together.

EXERCISES

The Semans Technique for Delaying Ejaculation

1. Masturbate until just before you reach the point of inevitability (the point when you know ejaculation is inevitable).

2. Stop and rest until you can take more stimulation without ejaculating.

3. Masturbate again until, once again, you reach a point just before the point of inevitability.

4. Stop and rest again until you can take more stimulation without ejaculating.

5. Masturbate, and stop and rest again. Then masturbate on through to ejaculation, if you wish.

6. Repeat steps one through five, four to six times a week for two weeks.

7. After two weeks, repeat the process using baby oil or Koromex II jelly or a body lotion, so that masturbation feels more like being inside the vagina: masturbating just up to the point before inevitability, stopping and resting, and repeating again.

In two more weeks you will find that it is beginning to take longer for you to reach the point of inevitability. You'll find that you'll be able to identify the point preceding inevitability with certainty. Not only will you find that it's taking you longer to reach orgasm, you'll also learn how to pace yourself.

When you make love, practice moving slowly and stopping. You might ask your partner to hold still for a while or slow down. You might also withdraw before the point of inevitability and rest before resuming intercourse. (It's important to point out that frequent practice helps. You may need to supplement intercourse with slow masturbation so you can practice delaying ejaculation several times a week.)

11

Saying Yes, Saying No, Saying Maybe

Imagine a world with no words.

Imagine a world where you could see and feel with great intensity, but could say nothing. How frustrating never to be able to say what you felt, tell what you saw, or share what you dreamed. You'd be reduced to grunting and moaning, rolling your eyes, humming, and sighing.

It may sound prehistoric, but that speechless world is an accurate description of most lovemaking scenes. Making love can be primitive but it doesn't have to be prehistoric.

Two people would never dream of making an omelet together without talking ("Two eggs or three? You use milk?"). A husband and wife assembling their child's toy the night before Christmas find speech natural and necessary ("Hold this for a second, will you, honey?" "Hey, wait a minute, you're holding that upside down"). And yet when they go hand in hand into the bedroom and begin to make love, an enterprise infinitely more shared, complex, and risky than making omelets or assembling toys, they stop talking.

Some people don't talk when they make love because they are shy, others because they are afraid that what they might say would sound awkward, out of place, or distracting. Many people feel as if their usual words aren't enough, as if there ought to be a new language, more exotic and exalted, to be spoken only while making love. But where could you learn that language? Talking is one part of lovemaking that sex manuals don't talk about. When movies show lovemaking, the soundtrack is full of music, not words. When people discuss their sex lives, they rarely mention what was said. Most people don't talk when they make love because most people have never learned how.

Lovemaking is shared; it is giving and taking. In some ways it is the ultimate communication between two people. There is so much to say: The intimate words of love and affection. Teaching your partner about your pleasures. Telling your partner about your sexual needs. Confiding your doubts and worries. Saying what you feel. Asking to be taught. Saying "no" or saying "yes." Saying "maybe."

Talking might just be the most varied, intimate, and neglected sexual technique of all.

What I'd like to describe here are some ways of being intimately assertive — ways of asking for what you want and expressing what you feel. Being assertive instead of passive while you are being intimate means that you are more likely to feel more pleasure.

First, you're more apt to get what you want, because you ask for it.

Next, being assertive inhibits anxiety just as pleasure inhibits anxiety. Feeling assertive is incompatible with feeling anxious. The more you feel the one, the less you will feel the other. So you can use assertive feelings to overcome anxiety just as you learned to use deep relaxation and erotic pleasure in chapters 4 and 5 to unlearn guilt and anxiety. Expressing assertive feelings enables you to overcome anxiety and learn assertiveness in its place. Here again, you need to begin with small amounts of anxiety, so that the assertive feelings can overpower the scary feelings.

Finally, saying what you want and what you feel can enhance intimacy.

Even before you begin lovemaking, it's important to be assertive. It's important to say what's on your mind, especially if there is something bothering you, something that threatens to raise a barrier between the two of you. Unsaid worries and unspoken anger usually don't go away. They just hide and come back to haunt you later.

Betty Anne, a forty-year-old architect, had a special, secret phone signal for her husband at his office. She'd ring once, hang up, and ring again. It was a signal she used to let him know she had something intimate to say. One day, when she was in her husband's office, she heard the same signal. As her husband talked on the phone, it was clear that he was talking to a junior executive about a marketing report. She didn't say anything, and her husband wondered for days why she was so cool to him in bed. She felt as if he had made their secret public, as if what was special and private to her wasn't any more special or private to him than a marketing report. "It was just a little thing," she said. "But it took me ten days to work up the courage to tell him how I felt. When I finally did tell him, I felt much better about him, and myself. And about making love again."

Judy, a twenty-six-year-old musician, covered up the jealousy she felt when her husband hugged another woman at a party. "It didn't seem important enough to mention," she said. "It seemed silly. But for the longest time, until I said what was on my mind, I went kind of blank sexually. When we made love, I felt as if he were touching someone else."

I mention these two examples to show that whatever is on your mind doesn't have to seem to be of major importance to have major consequences. If something is bothering you, don't hide it. Talk about it if you can. The sooner the better. If you feel some small resentment building up, or a need for something ("I need more romance," "I need more time with you"), or some discomfort, try to say so. These needs can be difficult to express. It takes both trust and intimacy to be able to discuss them.

The important thing is to take a first, tentative step, how-ever small, toward saying what you want and feel. You don't need to be clever or eloquent. If you can bring your worries or hesitations or desires out into the open, you can avoid the misunderstandings, resentments, and numbed feelings that are the penalty for silence. And if you can take just one small step, mentioning a small worry or just a part of a small worry, the assertiveness of doing that will help inhibit the anxiety you feel.

"I WANT TO MAKE LOVE WITH YOU"

The time to begin communicating in lovemaking is before you begin lovemaking. Of course there is a world of difference between having lived together for thirty years and never hav-ing been to bed together. Still, whether it is your first or your five thousandth time together, it is important to say what you mean rather than give vague signals. There are hundreds of ways to ask someone to make love. Some are clearly better than others. Better because they avoid misunderstanding and guesswork. The best, I think, are direct, caring, seductive, and romantic. Here are a few examples that, depending on the circumstances and how you say them, might fulfill all those requirements: "I want to make love with you." "Would you come to bed with me?" "Would you like to make love with me?"

It is important to ask instead of to assume. Assumptions clutter communication. And they are often so inaccurate.

Listen to just a few of the assumptions people make about their partners: "She wants to." "He doesn't really want me." "She's only holding back to tease me." "I'm pretty tired and feel crummy. But he wants to, so I guess we will." "I know he wants to 'cause he's got that gleam in his eyes." "Clean sheets! I guess she wants sex tonight." "The way she's kissing me means she wants to go all the way."

The answer to any sexual assumption is "Maybe." And "Maybe not." But after all, why guess? Why not just ask?

No matter how you ask, there's always the chance that you'll be rejected. And since rejection can be so painful, I'd like to suggest some ways of making rejection less painful.

"NO"

No is a strong word. It's not necessarily permanent. You can always change your mind. But there are times when "no" needs to be said: when you are tired, not in the mood, un-aroused, afraid of getting pregnant, feeling a lack of intimacy. Virtually all couples have frequency discrepancies, in which one wants to and the other doesn't. One wants to once a week, one wants to once a day. No two people are ever in perpetual synchronism in the rise and fall of their sexual desires.

You don't need to have a "good" reason for saying "no." And it is important to say "no" instead of "enduring" sex. Self-sacrifice in sex is not a virtue, it's a form of sexual suicide.

Saying "no" to having sex can be a very assertive and im-portant word to say. Instead of waiting until they feel over-whelmed with desire, many people have sex because they feel pressure to prove their virility, lose their virginity, or simply because they feel they "ought to." (If you don't feel ready for sex, if you don't feel there's intimacy and love, sex can inter-fere with a relationship and end it before it's had a chance to develop.)

Still, as important as it can be to say "no," how you say it may be even more important.

The problem is that for most couples, "no" sets up a neg-ative pattern. For example, a husband says, "Let's make love, honey." And a wife replies, "No." She feels guilty for saying "no." And he feels cold-shouldered, unappreciated, and re-jected. He gets a little angry at that, which makes her angry.

So now they're both angry and headed off in separate directions.

When "no" is interpreted as a personal rejection rather than a statement of mood or desire, there are apt to be hurt feelings. Let's look at some ways of saying "no" and of receiving a "no" that are less likely to make a partner feel rejected or angry. (These are part of a program I developed with Dr. William Kirby.)

Instead of just saying "no," you can offer a sensual alternative to intercourse: "No, but I'd like to kiss you." "No, but I'd like to touch you or have you touch me." "No, but I'd like to give you a massage." Or "No, but I'd like to give you a back rub."

There are other alternatives. "No, but I'd really enjoy lying here with you and talking." "No, but it would be nice if we could just read together." "No, I really care about you, but I'm just not in the mood."

You can say "I'm not sure." Many times you are not sure, and it's helpful to say so. "I'm not sure" is an especially important alternative for a woman. If may increase her "yeses." Many women are so used to taking their sexual cues from men that they don't recognize when they themselves are aroused. Many women don't become aroused before they become involved. So they say "no." But saying "I'm not sure, let's just kiss for a while" leaves time for your feelings to grow or languish until you are sure, one way or the other. You do, however, need to make it clear that saying "maybe" is not a tease — that it is entirely possible that the "maybe" will lead to a "no."

Another possibility is what Dr. Kirby calls a "caring compromise." If you don't feel in the mood for sex, and your lover feels very sexual, you might, by touching and kissing, help your partner to have sexual pleasure. As long as you feel no anxiety, you can give pleasure as an act of love, without negative consequences. Don't participate in a caring compromise if you feel any anxiety or resentment about what you are doing, or you may feel turned off by sex in the future.

The way you accept a "no" can be just as important as the way you say it. Accept a "no" lovingly and with empathy. Say: "I'm sorry that you're tired." "I am disappointed, because I desire you so much." "I love you. Could I just hold you in my arms as you go to sleep?" Accepting a "no" can be, as Lois Wyse says in her poem, "a gesture of love."

THE PERMISSIBLE NO

I said no
You turned
And kissed me very gently

And I felt an unexpected rush of love
How dear and sweet of you
To let me have my no
Without grim guilt

Did you know my dear
Or did you just this moment learn
The permissible no
Is a gesture of love.

"YES"

Oh yes. Yes indeed. Yes I do. Yes, I will, yes.

"Yes" can be the ultimate positive. The great affirmative. The one word you long to hear. The only word you want to say. The one word you're afraid to say. Especially if you've been told all your life to say "no."

In talking about intimate assertiveness I've taken some time to get to this one word, *yes*. And I want to spend some time on it. "Yes" comes in so many costumes, takes so many shapes and forms.

Yes doesn't have to be a permanent word. Just because

you've said "yes" once doesn't mean you have to continue to say it. That is particularly true if you're feeling uneasy about having sex with someone. You can always say "I said yes, but I don't feel right about it now. I guess I'm just not ready for sex with you. I care for you, but I think we've gone too quickly."

Starting back at the beginning can make for a marvelous, fresh start. Young people who come to me for counseling often assume that once you have sex with someone, it's an irreversible step, that the only way to stop the sexual part of a relationship is to end the whole relationship. What I usually suggest is that they step back, stop the sex, get to know each other better, and then wait and see.

Saying "yes" to having sex means that you accept the responsibility to teach and to learn. Nobody knows, automatically, how to make love with you. And you don't have any magical insight about how to make love with someone else. There are only guidelines. This book is full of them. But your own feelings and pleasures and your partner are the real guides. You have to communicate that you need your partner to teach you and that you need to teach your partner. If you're not accustomed to talking or asking or teaching while you make love, it may seem a little scary to begin, partly because you have never done it before and partly because you may feel so vulnerable in bed. One man, who is the chairman of his own company and on the board of directors of several others, confided to me that "never, in my whole life, am I so vulnerable as when I am in bed making love with my wife."

If you are hesitant to talk, if the first word seems to be a difficult, even dangerous step, you might try direct calming, using assertiveness and erotic feelings to calm your anxiety. When you are highly aroused, you will find it easier to begin to talk, because, as you know, pleasure reduces anxiety. So in the midst of feeling very sexual you might try something as simple as a murmur of pleasure, a soft, tentative groan, just to see how it feels. You might say a word or two of appreciation when something feels especially nice: "That's very good." "I like that." "That feels terrific." Proceed slowly and tentatively, step by step, until you are comfortable with asking your partner to "put your hand here," "do more," or groaning or sighing or simply saying "yes." Each step is reinforced by pleasure as long as pleasure wins and anxiety loses.

You might ask your partner to teach you about what is pleasurable for him or her. Asking to be taught can be a very tender part of lovemaking and a real adventure. There is so much variation from one person to another and in one person from one day to another that your past experience isn't a very reliable guide. What you want to communicate is that you need to be taught ("I'm not sure that I know how to touch you"). Or, for example, you can ask "Is that good?" It makes it easier for your partner to guide you if you can ask very specific questions. "How does it feel when I touch you here?" "Is that too firm?" or "Does this feel good?" "Too fast?" "Too slow?" "Softer?" "Harder?"

You might also invite your partner to guide your hand over his or her body, showing you how he or she likes to be touched. Part of learning is noticing subtle body movements and what they mean in terms of "more," or "less," or "harder," or "softer," or "yes, that's the place." One man was amazed at what a marvelous lover his wife had become. "Where did you learn all those great things to do?" he asked her. "From studying you very closely," she answered.

You can also take the lead and teach your partner how to please you. Put your hand on your partner's hands and guide them all over your body, holding them in one place where you'd like them to linger, and moving them on to another when you'd like. With a little practice, you can indicate if you'd like more pressure or less, rapid movements or slow. This is particularly useful for touching genitals, where subtle changes in pressure and rhythm can give you pleasure. An interesting variation of this technique is to put your hand *under* your partner's hand and as you touch yourself he or she can learn the subtleties of pressure and discover the hidden places that please you. You might feel too shy to touch yourself when you are with a partner. However, you can use direct calming in the midst of erotic feelings, guiding your partner's hand for a brief few moments, stopping if you feel any discomfort. And then you can do a bit more later. These are only suggestions, not laws of procedure. Still, placing your hand under your lover's hand is sometimes the only way you can show exactly how and when and where.

And, of course, the subtleties of stimulation can often be communicated verbally. You can say what you like and ask for what you want. You can say "yes" or "no" or "Ah, stay there for a while." You can say "I'd like you to kiss and touch me some more before we have intercourse." Instead of saying "Don't do that," which sounds negative, be more positive by suggesting another place or another way, moving your partner's hand and/or saying "I'd like you to touch my —— instead." Or "My back would be so grateful for a little attention now."

It's often a good idea to reassure your partner when you suggest another way or another place. If you find you need more time, for example, instead of saying "Slow down," you might be a little more gentle and say "I need more time. It's me, not you. You're wonderful. But I just need more time." It's also important to reassure your partner if you are having some difficulty. "You're very exciting, but I guess I'm also very tired." "I always take a long time to have an orgasm. I hope that's O.K." Humor, as I've described in chapter 9, can also help you through some of those awkward moments.

Intimate assertiveness includes talking about your fears, worries, and inhibitions. Almost everyone has them. And just saying you have them can lead a long way toward making them disappear — toward helping you feel less discomfort —

because assertiveness reduces anxiety. "I'm too scared to try oral sex." "I feel shy." "I'm worried that you won't like me in the nude." "I haven't done this before."

It's also tremendously helpful to your partner to learn about what frightens, pleases, and displeases you.

(By the way, while we're on the subject of being pleasing, it's O.K. to ask your partner to wash or bathe or shower before lovemaking. You can make it a very mild and gentle suggestion and part of your lovemaking, "Let's take a shower together first." Or you can be quite direct: "I'd like you to wash first.")

One of the important things to keep in mind is that it is not so much what you say or mean to say, but rather what your partner thinks you said that is the greatest measure of intimate communication. To keep what you meant and what your partner thought you meant as close as possible, and so enhance the pleasure, trust, and affection between you, I have five suggestions:

1. *No Put-downs*. It's inaccurate and hurtful to say "You're inadequate because you don't like your breasts touched," or "It's weird that you don't like oral sex," or "That's a dumb thing to want to do." Put-downs can make your partner feel defensive and insecure. And you won't feel any better for them, either.

2. *Praise*. Everyone likes praise when it's real. It's good to hear "That's good," "I like the way you do that," "I feel good in your arms," "You're so good," and "You have the nicest way of touching me." The technical term for this form of encouragement is positive reinforcement. And it's something you should do outside lovemaking as well, particularly in a long-term relationship, in which you tend to take each other for granted. Praise and thank-yous don't have to be lavish to be important. "You look really good this morning," "I admired the way you handled yourself," and "Thank you for leaving me a note telling me where you'd gone" are the kinds of state-

ments that keep a relationship warm and loving. And the trust and affection they encourage can carry over into bed.

3. *No Guessing.* Guessing and making assumptions about another person's sexual feelings have a very low accuracy rate. There are just too many variables and too many possibilities to know precisely what another person is thinking and feeling. Besides, there are no universals in sex. Change may be the only constant. Here are some examples of mistaken assumptions and wrong guesses: "All women like having their breasts caressed." "He'll think I mean 'yes' if I let him touch me." "He won't be patient enough for me to really get to enjoy his touching my clitoris." "She thinks my penis is too small." "I must be doing something wrong."

Of course, there's a chance your guess may be right. But why guess? Ask, if you want to know and be sure.

4. *Say "I."* Instead of saying "You hurt me," say "I feel hurt." "I feel," "I want," "I'd like" can all be straightforward statements of what you think and feel. Saying "I" eliminates guesswork about why and who is to blame. By saying "I" you take responsibility for what you feel, and you avoid the tedious debates ("No, I didn't." "Yes, you did") that flare up when you make an accusation. Say "I need more affection" instead of "You don't give me enough affection." "You don't give me enough touching" implies inadequacy, breaks intimacy, and sounds accusing. "I'd like you to touch me more" is a statement of your needs.

5. *No "shoulds."* It's tempting to try to improve someone by scolding. "You shouldn't go so fast," "You should do more ——," "You should be more sensual" are all negative, discouraging statements. If you want to change someone's lovemaking, you can say what you want and need without making demands such as saying "you should." Use "I" statements (from number 4 above) and compliment your partner for the things that he or she does well. Habits are deeply ingrained. And people are slow to change. Changes in love-

making take patience, intimacy, and understanding. And they come about through emphasizing your partner's strengths, not criticism. Saying "you should do this" or "you shouldn't do that" puts a damper on intimacy and a barrier to change, as it builds resentment.

*

Lovemaking is shared, two people joining as closely as possible. Communication is one of the strongest links that joins. It is the basis for understanding. A special touch, a sigh of pleasure, a word of love, a cry of ecstasy — these are all elements of intimate communication.

I cannot say what you should say or how you should caress. For the language of your lovemaking is not mine, but yours. Discovering those words and caresses is what you and your lover will do when you next make love. My hope is that what I have outlined here will help make those discoveries of your own words and caresses easier, more frequent, and delicious.

PART THREE

SHARING

---

*At heart this book is as much about
love as it is about sex.*

You know so much more now; now that you are
free from old fears and ties, now that you can
communicate and laugh in the bedroom. Now you
are ready for the exploration, risk, and adventure,
the unexpected and sometimes beautiful discoveries that are possible when you can trust enough
to be accepting and vulnerable.

12

A Sensual Holiday

Somewhere in the world, no doubt, someone is sick of caviar and champagne, bored with sunshine and rain, and fed up with the same old yachts.

No pleasure is forever, for pleasures are the shadows of time. Pleasures blaze and dance for a moment, then time moves on. The moment disappears and the pleasures are gone. You can go back, but you can't go back very often. Time and people change. Repetition wears pleasure down. The same time, the same place, the same way, and the same face.

No pleasure could possibly survive the dictatorial regime of habit wherein people (after they've settled down) confine their sexual celebrations. Sometimes I imagine a crescendo of TV clicks around 11:30 p.m. all across the country as couples turn off the late-night news and begin to creak the bedsprings. It is the North American mating hour, when everyone is tired and worn. Same time, same place, same way, same tired, sleepy face.

The insidious thing about sexual boredom is not just that it creeps up slowly, or that it happens to almost every couple who spend years together, or that nobody talks about it. No, the insidious thing is that most people assume that sexual boredom is a sign of something else, something more than just boredom. Couples, when they run into sexual boredom, tend to feel that their relationship is breaking up, or that their partner has found someone else, or that they themselves are inadequate. All of the above are possible, but unlikely. It's more likely that they are in a rut, a repetitive habit that has taken place so often they always know what is going to happen next. Life or sex without surprise is boring, but not incurable. Still, people search for other "causes."

Belinda and Jack had been married for two years. They were loving and kind toward each other. But they were concerned that a lot of the magic had gone out of their lovemaking. Making love used to be a major event before they were married. Sometimes they spent weeks just planning what weekends she could get away to spend at his college, what weekends he could spend at hers. Their early courtship had been by long-distance telephone, with a few weekends together in the New England fall and winter. Sometimes a month of longing and anticipation would crawl by until they could be together. Now, living in the same apartment, with sex a constant possibility, they wondered what was wrong.

I suggested that they take a sensual holiday. Jack, in his Brooks Brothers tweed sport jacket, pulled back his shoulders and said I wasn't "speaking to the issue." He felt that there had to be some "critical flaw" in their relationship, something more than just being in a rut, that needed to be "understood." He was sure that a sensual holiday would not be helpful.

When they left they were just as discouraged about their relationship as when they came in.

Three weeks later, they were back.

They had driven down the coast to visit Belinda's parents. In the early-morning hours when they arrived, they discovered they'd forgotten their keys. Belinda's mother wasn't well, the night was warm, and rather than wake the elderly woman, they folded back the seats of the car and snuggled together and made love. "It was just so *good*," said Jack with great seriousness. "Better than good," said Belinda. "It was sensational."

By a happy coincidence, they had discovered the truth of what I had told them.

A sensual holiday is an hour, a day, or a week when you leave your old routines and roles behind, and begin again to teach and to learn how to be intimate. It's a way of bringing the feeling of summer evenings into winter days, of putting cares and worries into a distant perspective, of celebrating each other — of stopping the world, getting off and having a look in another direction.

Along with Dr. William Kirby, I developed the concept of a sensual holiday to put passion and romance back into a long-term relationship, to heighten excitement and add adventure; to give people a chance to be playful, loving, and human, to try new things, to improve their sexual communication and escape from the tyranny of their old habits and agendas.

In other words, a sensual holiday is a vacation from your everyday life, when you devote yourself to sensuality and intimacy. It's also a time for introducing some changes into your sexual routine. And it's a time to learn how to be romantic.

As Belinda and Jack discovered in their car, three hundred miles from home, a sensual holiday can happen any time, anyplace. But you can't depend on chance. Usually the world won't go away unless you arrange for its departure.

PLANNING

You might take turns being in charge of and planning a sensual evening or weekend. Once you start planning a sensual holiday, you'll find that arranging to do what you want to do helps develop your assertiveness as well as build anticipation and desire. It also affects your "to do" list; for example, amongst the everyday shopping items are erotic flowers, such as "buy lace panties," blooming with the promise of pleasure.

Getting started, taking the first step toward a sensual holiday, isn't always easy. Elaine is anything but shy about suggesting sexual adventures to her live-in lover, Gene. But she has an idea that might prove useful to even the shyest of lovers — coupons. From time to time, at dinner or breakfast, she hands Gene an envelope with a hand-drawn coupon inside. Sometimes she mails them to him at his office. The coupons are redeemable at any mutually agreed upon time. Let me give you a sample of some of Elaine's coupons.

- One bubble bath for two.
- One intimate dinner (dress will be optional).
- One fondle and three feels in the back of a taxi.
- One evening in a fancy hotel.
- One slippery massage.
- Ten minutes of petting in the back row of a movie theater.
- One evening of total submission to your wishes.
- One afternoon delight.
- One breakfast in bed.
- One sexual fantasy performed (sorry, no whips).
- One champagne evening in bed.
- One weekend away from it all.
- One sexually explicit phone call.

You might also begin by issuing an invitation. "You are cordially invited to dessert and champagne for two. Dress will be scanty. And I shall be in charge."

Some of the best sensual holidays involve all of your senses. A weekend, for example, might include art galleries or movies or walks in the forest, a picnic on a hilltop, dinner at a special restaurant, a concert or a play, the scent of flowers, the deep relaxation of a massage, an evening dinner at a hotel of just hors d'oeuvres or desserts in bed. You might even plan to spend a whole day in bed. The point is to involve and indulge all your senses, so that, for a time at least, you become creatures of pleasure and romance.

As I mentioned, part of the reason for a sensual holiday is to introduce change into your lovemaking. Change is the renewing force of nature. Seasons and tides, moons and suns, come and go, rise and fall. All living things change. The creatures that cannot change, like dinosaurs, die. Lovemaking without change loses the life and spirit it once had.

The first two changes I would suggest in planning a sensual holiday are time and place.

If you usually make love at a certain time, change it. You might meet in the afternoon, in the morning, or plan to make love in the early-morning hours. Changing the time instantly jostles old routines and gives everything you do a sense of newness.

Changing the place adds adventure. Your bedroom, bower though it may be, is only one place to make love. There are also the kitchen, the dining room, and the bathtub. One student couple were nimble enough to make love in the bathroom of a Pan Am jet. You might consider borrowing a friend's apartment, going to a romantic hotel, finding a clearing in the forest, taking a blanket to the dunes at the beach, making love in a barn or even a corner office. Some people find that the risk of being discovered adds intensity. But for most people (particularly when they are trying something new), privacy is tremendously important. One couple engineered their privacy by turning on the shower while they made love, so their visiting uncle in the next room couldn't hear their groans and howls. You may want to go a step further and send the kids to your mother's or to a friend's house for the weekend. Engineering your own privacy can be as simple as putting a lock on your bedroom door, or making sure the do-not-disturb sign is displayed outside the hotel room. For if you are on a sensual holiday, you will want to be making worlds of your own, spontaneously, playfully, without the interrupting concerns of the irrelevant remainder of the human race.

Besides changing the time and the place, you might also ask for something new. You might ask to have your back rubbed or your hair stroked. It might be "I've always wanted to make love on the beach. Would you like to try that?" Or "I wonder if it'd be good to make love standing up." Notice that the request is tentative, not demanding. "I wonder how you'd feel about keeping the lights on. I've always wanted to."

THINGS TO DO

First, you might set the scene and arrange the mood. Candlelight and flowers, music and wine are so obvious it's easy to forget how romantic they are in the bedroom. The warm and flickering light of candles casts shadows, and gives a sensual and warm glow to lovers — a half light in which your sense of touch becomes your second sight. Music adds as much rhythm and mood as you choose. Mirrors, while they are more difficult to arrange than candles, can be just as sensual. Seeing yourself and your lover caressing each other, seeing your lover in the mirror undressing, seeing the two of you making love — mirrors can be a magical reflection, especially with flowers and candlelight. You might also tell your partner what you'd like him or her to wear, particularly underwear.

Ah, underwear. One petite green-eyed bank manager has been investing in an extensive portfolio of silks, satins, laces, and tricot. Beneath her banker's tweeds she is apt to wear an outrageous bra. Sensual lingerie feels so delicious to wear, feels so good to feel, and adds so much that you just might consider buying something new for the occasion.

If you're wearing a bra, you might take it off when you're making out, but leave on a soft sweater, a silk blouse, or a revealing dress. Dinner and dancing, by yourselves, half dressed, can set a richly erotic mood. Alternatively, if you're dining out, a woman might just whisper to her partner as they whisk past the doorman "I'm not wearing any panties."

If you or your lover has a special erotic desire for, say, black bikini panties, or high-heeled boots, or wearing a football jersey to bed, a sensual holiday is the time to try out those desires. You need a sense of humor and a good deal of understanding. After all, whims may not work just the way you had imagined. Still, a sensual holiday is for trying out something you've always wanted to do but never tried before.

Wherever and whenever you begin your sensual holiday, I'd suggest that sometimes you begin with a ban on intercourse. Agree that for several hours or the night or the weekend you will not have intercourse. I know it may be difficult to abstain. But a ban builds up excitement, tantalization, and pleasure. And when you both decide later that you can't wait any longer, that intercourse is irresistible, and you break the ban, that's fine. Breaking the ban almost adds to the enjoyment. And it's very different from thinking "Tonight's the night. And I'm going to do it, no matter what." Putting a ban on something sexual can lower your anxiety and increase your pleasure. You might say it's like putting the lid on a cookie jar. It makes you hungry for what you cannot have. It encourages you to find pleasure elsewhere, in places you may not have thought of before. A ban on touching genitals, for example, leads you to seek pleasure in caressing other parts of your bodies. And a ban on taking off clothes can be incredibly tantalizing.

Even more than heightening pleasure or building anticipation and desire, a ban on intercourse can take the focus off intercourse as the "goal" of your lovemaking. If you can let your lovemaking become less linear, random almost, you're much more apt to discover new pleasures and delights. And when you discover new pleasures you'll also be more likely to take your time, to enjoy and savor them, instead of brushing your new discoveries aside as you rush to intercourse.

A sensual holiday can begin almost anywhere, but one of the most sensual places is the bathtub. Possibly it's the warmth of the water, the sensation of the smooth soap. Whatever the reason, taking a bath (or shower) together seems to bring out the water nymph and satyr in almost everyone. (It's bound to be awkward, too, and a little silly. So you have to be able to laugh.) Knees up and sloshing around, you're in a steamy pleasure boat for teasing and rubbing. Wash each other all over with your hands. You might try a special soap or bubble bath. Giving each other shampoos is nice. And so is slow and slippery caressing of breasts and genitals. Each person can take turns being totally pampered by the other. For an ending, you can lovingly and carefully towel each other off, and rub talcum powder or after-bath lotion all over each other.

In the warm glow and languor after a bath together, you might just laze and luxuriate in the comfort of each other's arms, listen to records, or read. A sensual holiday doesn't have to be a constant procession of sexual activities. After all, it is a vacation from pressure and worry, so you can relax and be loving.

You might also try seduction.

Seduction can be a delicious new game. It's especially good for women who are used to being passive in sex. Seduction can be a fine turn-on, a chance to be assertive, with words and gestures, teasings and come-ons (not teasing to hurt, teasing to enhance arousal), music, dancing for someone, stripping someone, stripping for someone. You'll need a sense of humor to do a seductive strip, because there are bound to be zippers that stick or snaps that won't snap or awkward moments that find you hopping on one foot. Still it can be surprisingly erotic.

The Striptease

1. Music helps.
2. The point of a strip is to be tantalizing and teasing, so don't just take your things off, reveal yourself slowly. You can take off one bra strap, pause for a while, and then take off the other. You might take off your panties before you take off your skirt. Then, pull up your skirt, slowly, teasingly, and let it down again. You can take time, while you're halfway through a strip, to brush your hair, slowly and sensually.
3. Keep your distance for a while. Pose under a soft light

across a darkened room. You might come very close to your partner, letting him know that he can look but he can't touch. In posing in the half shadows across the room or very close to your lover, you might think of yourself as the most beautiful model in the world, posing for a photographer, arching your back, stretching out a leg, or slowly turning to reveal that you are touching yourself. Not only does posing look sensual, but it also gives you the sense of your own body being an instrument of pleasure. As you are posing and stripping, you'll find yourself moving more sinuously, carrying yourself erect, with pride. Feeling good about your pleasure and the pleasure you can give influences the way you carry yourself in and out of lovemaking.

4. You might take off a bra or camisole and fling it across the room. (Flings are great fun in strips.)

5. As an extra, erotic touch, after taking off your silky slip or satin panties, caress your partner with your sensual lingerie. The texture and erotic associations can be very arousing.

6. From time to time, run your hands over your legs and breasts, over your stomach and arms. Feel how good it feels to touch yourself all over. Focus on the texture of your silky lingerie and the warmth and softness of your skin.

7. When you have taken most of your clothes off, you might consider leaving a few things on for a while. A garter belt and stockings, for example. (Once upon a time, in Victorian music halls and bedrooms, the merest glimpse of a garter belt on a feminine thigh made gentlemen forget they were gentlemen. This now nearly vestigial satin accessory must have made quite an impact. There are still men who claim the visual effect of a woman wearing nothing but garters and stockings is so erotic it should be against the law.)

8. Then there are pearls. There's a classical innocence about pearls gracing a woman's neck that belies their erotic possibilities. Perhaps it's their smoothness, the way they are warmed by the skin, that makes them so sensual. Certainly you might consider leaving your pearls on after you are nude.

Later, when you are kissing and caressing, you might take off your pearls, caress your lover's body with them, wrap them around your lover's penis, and roll them up and down the shaft of the penis. You can also wrap them around his testicles. The feeling, it is reported by some, is exquisite.

A Lover's Massage

Take turns massaging each other all over, rubbing the forehead, temples, legs, or between the shoulder blades to relieve tension and be affectionate. Incidentally, you might try using mineral oils or some lightly scented body oils for a massage.

It's important that you develop communication between you as you touch, so that your partner can tell you what's good and what's not so good. Part of a sensual holiday is teaching each other to focus on sensuality and learning to de-emphasize performance. For example, touch and kiss your partner solely for your own pleasure. This is a chance to touch and feel and kiss wherever you like — to try a little massaging, to trace a vein, and so on. Your partner has an obligation to tell you if you make him or her tense or uncomfortable. Once you know that — that your partner will stop you if he or she doesn't like something that you are doing — you can feel entirely free to explore and enjoy.

Next, try giving as much pleasure as humanly possible. The other person has to help you do this by teaching you how and where, how firm or gentle, how long or soft a stroke, when and how and where he or she likes to be kissed. That puts all the responsibility on the teacher (the person who's getting the pleasure) for getting the utmost pleasure. When it's your turn to teach, make believe you are the queen of England or the king of France and you want and deserve as much pleasure as possible. You can teach verbally and nonverbally. You can put your hands on the other person's hands to guide them, indicating where, how, and how firmly. Or simply tell your partner what you wish or guide your partner's head to where you'd like to be kissed.

The third activity is to focus on what you feel, to become acutely aware of the temperature and texture under your fingers. You might focus on whether the place you are touching is smooth or warm or moist or cool or rough. You might also focus on signs of pleasure in your partner, such as rapid breathing or subtle body movements.

You can use these same techniques of massage and sensual awareness on the genitals for an erotic massage. Baby oil or a nonscented (perfume can be an irritant) body lotion on genitals feels especially nice, because these liquids can intensify sensation.

A massage, even an erotic massage, doesn't have to lead to intercourse. A massage doesn't have to be something you do on the way to something else, but rather for its own sake, for the pleasure it gives you and your partner. In that spirit, outside the pressures of time and performance, not heading in any one direction but exploring where the mood and pleasures lead you, you can take all the time you like and be an adventurer on the verge of discovery.

There is so much to discover. A sensual holiday is a chance to try out a sexual fantasy you've always wanted to try, to make love on a beach, try out a new position, a water bed, or satin sheets. (I'll discuss ways to act out fantasies in the next chapter. For the moment I'll just mention that with fantasies as with anything else new sexually, you should proceed slowly and gradually, one step at a time.) You can tentatively try some of the sexual techniques and variations from other chapters. You can expand your sexual communication. And you can escape from old sexual habits that may have made sex routine.

Most important, you can develop that sense that draws you out and makes you larger than yourself: intimacy. Sexual confidence is that sense of possibility, humility, and greatness that comes from the closest of all human relationships, intimacy.

13

Being Intimate

I have a confession to make.

At heart, this book is as much about love as it is about sex. Sex without love is, after all, only sex. Without love, sex may be playful, pleasurable, erotic, and breathtaking. It may be any number of things. But it will certainly be finite, defined by the limits of sensation.

Sex at its best is a way of expressing love, of making *love*. When sex is charged with love, the barriers to sensation are down and the possibilities are wide open.

Whatever you feel love is — and everybody seems to have his or her own definition — I would guess that your definition is somewhat vague. Most of us, after all, like to include everything we can in our definition of love. On the other hand, that vagueness, that all-inclusive generality, makes it seem almost impossible to "learn" love. Most people would say that love is something that just happens — the way lightning strikes.

What you have been doing in these chapters is learning ways of loving — ways of loving yourself and others. Some of the ways are earthy. Fine. Love isn't all abstracts. The amazing nearness of another passionate being, naked and kissing you on the neck, is anything but abstract.

Yet the temptation, when the subject of love comes up, is to wander off into romantic or religious abstracts. Those abstractions ("Love is all," "Love is the cosmos," "God is love") make it seem difficult to learn the specifics of love. For while they sound fine and may be true, how can such massive concepts help young lovers develop their love beyond heart throbs or save a faltering marriage? Part of human love *is* mysterious and magical, and beyond our control. At the same time, the single most important part of human love is intimacy. You can create and develop intimacy. Intimacy can be learned. Through intimacy you can make love grow.

Intimacy is a holiday from the solitary churnings of your mind; a safe, comfortable place where you can let down your guard and put aside the armor you wear for the world. Intimacy is talking late at night, after the lights are out, sharing stories of old friends and good times, and making new plans. Intimacy is comparing notes on your corner of the universe, laughing together, feeling sad together for what might have been, and hoping for what still could be. Intimacy is building an afternoon or a life together, sharing the passage of time.

The warmth and love you feel in intimacy has an extra dimension. As intense and realistic as your own experience may be, it is still a singular point of view — the thoughts, feelings, and sensations of one person. When you add the dimension of intimacy — sharing and accepting another person's experience and point of view — the result is more than one-plus-one. For this resonance and perspective adds amazingly to your own sense of life and love. It's the difference between seeing with one eye and two, between a flat world and a world of solid shapes and depth. It is the difference between single-speaker sound and stereo, in which the background and foreground separate in relative importance and the details of the music are clear, and the harmony and the melody and the rhythm are no longer single notes on a single line but elements of space.

Of course, intimacy is worth having. The question is, how

does one have it? The first step is to recognize that beyond mystery and magic, intimacy is being accepting and being vulnerable.

Here we are at the nub of love. And this is the most difficult part of sexual confidence, the step that is the hardest to take. All your life you have been taught to be self-sufficient and strong. Even Mother Nature makes that lesson clear. Being strong and independent, fulfilling your own needs, and being able to weather emotional storms are valuable, positive traits to bring into a relationship. But the ability to let down your guard is a prerequisite of love — a risk you can take only when you feel totally accepted. In the paradox of intimacy the things that seem like weaknesses are often the real strengths.

If you can feel accepted, you don't have to pretend to be strong when you're not. Your fears can be soothed and your worries brought down to size. Acceptance gives your love a reality and beauty that it otherwise would not have.

ACCEPTANCE

Acceptance happens slowly. After the first rush of love or passion, the irritations emerge. Yesterday's silky tresses clog the sink. A husky voice rasps. A free spirit seems irresponsible on Monday morning. A great intellect anchors Saturday night in gloom.

It's hard to accept someone else's faults. Heaven knows, it's hard enough to accept your own. Total acceptance is very rare. Perhaps only saints can do it. Still, it's a useful goal and worth aiming at.

You accept someone because you love them and because you want to share intimacy with that person. You accept their opinions, foibles, and fears as you accept their eyes and kisses. Accepting doesn't mean that you agree with everything a person thinks or does; rather, you accept their thoughts and actions as part of the person you love.

See how the circle goes:

The more you accept me, the more I can accept myself. The more I can accept myself, the more I can risk being vulnerable with you. The more vulnerable I am with you, the more you can trust me. The more we trust each other, the more intimacy we share. The more intimacy we share, the more love we have. And the more I love you, the more I accept you.

You can get on that loving-go-round at almost any point. But the easiest way to begin is by being accepting.

Being accepting means giving empathy instead of criticism.

Lillian, dean of students at an Eastern college, comes home many nights exhausted from the demands of students, faculty, and administrators. Her husband, Charles, doesn't say "You shouldn't work so hard" or "You shouldn't let those people get to you like that." Instead he gives her hugs, listens to her, and empathizes with her, sometimes cooks supper and often gives her flowers. After she has faced conflict all day, Charles's kindness and acceptance give Lillian the rest and reassurance she needs to "go forth and do battle." For when you have acceptance in intimacy, you don't need as much praise and approval from the outside world.

If you are accepted in love, you don't have to prove yourself. If you are accepted for who you are and not for who you could be or should be, there's no need for pretenses, or trying to prove how brave, smart, rich, athletic, or sexual you are. Acceptance lets you be yourself. The invitation reads "Come as you are."

Knowing that what you think and feel won't be put down by your lover gives you the freedom to think and feel more deeply and intensely. You can be irrational, so that what might seem to be weakness to the outside world (a man crying) becomes the shared strength of deep emotion.

With acceptance you begin to feel comfortable taking emotional and sexual risks. When you try something new in sex, there are bound to be missed cues and false starts. After all, you are learning. With acceptance, the learning and the ad-

venture can lead to beauty instead of a sense of failure. Acceptance gives you the courage to accept the risk of sexual prat-
falls as the price you pay for attempting great leaps.

The art of being accepting, though, is in taking small,
accepting steps, not great leaps. You may have to take hundreds of them. There is so much to accept.

Acceptance is granting the people you love their right to be
human — their inalienable right to their own flaws. It's loving
not just their most attractive traits, but also their least attractive ones. After the first highs of romance you begin to notice
the refrigerator door has been left open yet again. Dirty socks
litter the carpet. He squanders money. She is always late. He
drives too fast. She doesn't like sex in the morning. He ejaculates too soon. She is overprotective of the children. He flirts
with your friends. She watches too much television. There's
worse. There's more. But instead of listing all your lover's
faults and adding them up, begin with just one flaw and accept it. You can certainly speak about it and say how much
it annoys you: "I have to tell you, Frank, I hate seeing the
ashtrays full of your pipe ashes." But you also need to add, on
this "trial" flaw acceptance: "On the other hand, I love you,
and pipe ashes are part of the man I love."

Acceptance can be very difficult. But just for practice, take
one small irritation and instead of fighting it, instead of letting
it irritate you more each time you notice it, see if you can relax
and accept it. The reason you want to start with something
small — that is, something that doesn't irritate you much —
is that you need to be sure that your love wins out over your
annoyance.

Some things are easier to accept than others. Some people
don't mind a messy bedroom. Others demand military pre-
cision in sheets. Eating habits can be loaded with conflict:
"Good grief, you're not using sugar/salt/fat, are you?" Accept the small irritations first, one at a time, and the larger
areas are apt to diminish in importance.

(On the other hand, if you find serious, even destructive

areas of conflict — if you find, for example, that your lover is an alcoholic, a compulsive gambler, a constant and severe critic, nonsexual, or, to be less dramatic, can talk only about money — you may also find there is only so much that *can* be accepted. It may be better to end a destructive relationship than to prolong it.)

Acceptance is easiest when you see how closely it is related to friendship.

In a sense, acceptance is a fancy word for friendship. Romance attracts, friendship holds. Romance is the perfume and spice of intimacy; friendship is the cement. Lovers rarely stay lovers without friendship. Friendship is praising strengths instead of criticizing weaknesses. Friendship is being there when you are needed, helping to fight your partner's battles, and soothing your partner's wounds.

In another sense, friendship is the nonsexual side of intimacy — sharing your experiences, plans, hopes, and frustrations. Friendship cushions you against the inevitable fall off those first ecstatic high peaks of early romance. If there is a strong bond of friendship between you, you can accept the lows along with the highs.

Acceptance and friendship are effective antidotes to the impossible expectations of the Cinderella myth. (You remember the Cinderella myth: Somewhere someone perfect waits for me. Our perfect love will always be perfect.) Friendship helps you accept the fact that Prince Charming tells the same old horse stories over and over, or that Cinderella never sweeps the hearth. Friendship helps you accept and love Cinderella even when she's no longer the belle of the ball. And friendship helps you accept and love Prince Charming when he's given up his throne to be a king among pumpkins.

If you can accept just one small flaw as a part of the person you love, your love will grow that one step.

Acceptance leads to vulnerability. You have to feel you will be accepted, you have to trust your partner, before you can expose the vulnerable sides of yourself.

BEING VULNERABLE

"Be open" is common advice from many professionals in my field. But I cannot give you a blanket instruction to "be open," because openness can lead to pain. It is important to exercise discretion in being open, to go slowly, sharing your vulnerabilities one step at a time. As hard as it may be to feel acceptance and be accepting, being vulnerable is even more difficult. As you will see, there is a direct, positive relationship between how vulnerable you can be and how much you can love and be loved. But that doesn't make being vulnerable any easier.

It's not easy to admit to an outrageous desire, or to be irrational, sad, silly, or wrong in an intimate relationship when in other relationships the world penalizes any admission of less than perfection. Saying you're depressed at work, or that you're scared to go into a big meeting, doesn't get you big raises. And if you've had a painful ending to the last time you were in love, it can be terribly difficult to "admit" how much you care and to "confess" how much you need.

Vulnerability means exposing all the sides of yourself. That means taking real risks. The reward of vulnerability is more love. As the risk and the reward are tangled together, let's look at them both.

To some degree we would all like to be perfect. Failing that, it might be nice to appear to be perfect, or at least better than you think you are. And to maintain the falsehood, to hide your less appealing aspects, you close off part of yourself. The more you close off, the more invulnerable you are and the less you will feel. On the other hand, the more you disclose of yourself, the more intensely you will be able to feel. This is where risk and reward become tangled together. For in being vulnerable you are laying yourself open to pain as well as to love. You are more easily hurt by someone who knows where your soft spots are. So there is wisdom in going slowly, disclosing just one vulnerability at a time ("I feel shy with you," "I need more time with you," "I sort of fold up when I'm criticized"). See how the person reacts. If your vulnerabilities are met with advice, criticism, moralizing, or hostility, you will have lost a little, not a lot. And you can stop. But if each step of disclosing a vulnerability ("I'm not very brave," "I am lonely for you") is met with kindness and warmth ("I'm glad you told me that," "I know what you mean," "I want to be with you when you cry, not just when you're happy"), you can venture another step. Incidentally, when someone tells you his or her problems, you don't have to fix those problems for them. What you can do is listen and empathize.

I doubt that letting yourself be vulnerable is ever easy. But the reward for taking each courageous step is greater intimacy and more intense feelings. Because when you are vulnerable with someone you allow yourself to be closer to that person. You also allow him/her to be close to you. The reason is simple enough. Along with our need to be loved and to love we also need to be needed. Loving a totally invulnerable person, a person who doesn't seem to need your love, is about as rewarding as loving a wall. But when the person you love becomes vulnerable to you, you feel needed. You try to protect their vulnerabilities and shield that person from pain. Often it's the fears and incompleteness that bring out your love most.

Jean, a successful advertising executive, was very strong and self-confident. Her strength and toughness were a real asset in her job, where she was often the only woman in a room full of anxious, competing executives. She felt, she said, she had to be stronger than any of them to survive. But she found that when she carried her emotional toughness into her private life, her private life suffered. What had worked in the business world didn't work at home. Being invulnerable numbed her feelings. She wanted to be loving and "soft" with her husband, but until she could admit some of her fears and weaknesses it was almost impossible to feel loving. Until she could admit to being vulnerable, her husband didn't feel needed. As I said, it's a paradox. In intimacy, strong men and women cry. Out of vulnerability can come strength — a more intense love.

Often the stronger people appear, the more difficult it is for them to be vulnerable, since being vulnerable appears to threaten their strength.

Keith, a forty-four-year-old TV reporter, on and off the screen was "the anchorman," unruffled by national disasters. He seemed so much a monument to the strong, silent type, his colleagues sometimes called him "chief." Once when Keith was away from home, on assignment, Jennifer, his lover, overheard a conversation about an affair he had had six months before. Jennifer was devastated. Her first reaction was to try to cut herself off from her feelings. She was outraged that she was so vulnerable — so much more hurt than she would have expected. She had always felt "in control" of her feelings. Now she felt helpless. She decided she would end the affair rather than be so vulnerable to pain again. So she told Keith, on the phone, that they could no longer be lovers. Keith drove all night to be home in the morning. He said, in effect, "I'm ashamed, I was wrong. It was a very confusing time in my life. I don't know if you can forgive me. I'm not asking you to forgive me, but I want you to know I love you." Keith and Jennifer both wept. Keith wasn't the "strong, silent" man at that moment. He was simply human. And Jennifer didn't shut herself off from what she felt.

Although being vulnerable was painful, the depth of renewal that they both felt was intense and very loving. As Jennifer said, "It was like falling in love all over again."

Then there is the vulnerability of your secrets. Being vulnerable means you are able to take the risk of saying what you have never dared to tell anyone before. When you feel enough trust you might try telling your partner about a time when your parents rejected you, or when you cheated on a high-school test, or stole money off your father's dresser, or were an outcast in the seventh grade.

Being vulnerable isn't just admitting weakness or confessing transgressions. (In fact, confessions of former love affairs or details of former marriages are rarely, if ever, a good idea.)

Being vulnerable really means letting your emotions show, even when they seem at odds with the world. For a man to say "I'm too tired tonight" is an act of courage, given the macho stereotypes. It may even be sexually endearing.

There are also your sexual secrets — "I'm afraid you'll think this is kinky, but what I'd like to do now is ——," ' "I've always had this secret desire to ——." Sexual vulnerabilities are statements of strength when they are accurate reports of your wants and feelings: "I'd like to just caress. I'm not really in the mood for making love." "I'm scared to try oral sex." "I'd like to have an orgasm." "I want to give you more pleasure." "I'd like to last longer." In fact, one of the best measures of the strength of intimacy is how well a couple can handle sexual vulnerabilities.

INTIMATE GESTURES

The phone was made for lovers. Call when your lover is down and worried, to say good night, to congratulate or commiserate before or after a crucial event, just to be sexy, to say good morning, or after making love. Call to say "I love you." A phone call can be an instant electronic extension of romance, a way to be loving across a country, a mountain range, or a street.

Then there is the dramatic gesture, like Keith's four-hundred-mile drive through the night. Everyday life doesn't usually afford such opportunities, but you can make the effort, for example, to meet someone at the airport or train station instead of saying "See you when you get here." Any home-coming, even if it's just from a day at the office, can be cause for celebration. A flower on the table, a kiss, a warm hug can be eloquent ways of saying "I'm glad you're here."

And then, too, as a giver of acceptance and vulnerability it is important to recognize those gifts when they are given to you, and to say "I love you when you tell me these things," "It's so good when you share yourself with me." Giving compliments increases both intimacy and communication. "I love your sexuality" can be a reassuring, intimate statement from a woman to a man with a large sexual appetite. "I like the way you're doing that" can be tremendously reassuring to hear.

Of all that you share in intimacy, perhaps nothing is more intimate than fantasy.

SHARING FANTASY

Most lovers operate on at least one level of fantasy. Corporate presidents, chiefs of staff, All-Pro linebackers, and tax account-ants might be, respectively, "pussy cat," "sweetie," "dump-ling," or "super-stud" in the privacy of their homes.

Sharing a fantasy can be the height of intimacy. Fantasies are your most secret, guarded, and vulnerable thoughts. Many people fear to disclose their fantasies, because they think they are "weird" or "abnormal." But there is, short of obsession and physical harm, no such thing as an abnormal fantasy.

Fantasy is a chance to play, to indulge yourself and your partner in pleasure. There's an innocence in fantasy, a win-ning foolishness that dares to be silly or ridiculous. Yet be-cause fantasies are so private, you need trust to share them. You need to enter into and share fantasies cautiously, one step at a time.

For example, if you wish to share a sexual fantasy with your lover, you might begin by mentioning just one aspect of the fantasy. A woman might begin "I've always wanted to make love wearing silk stockings," and, as with any vulnerability, see how it is received. You are delivering your most defenseless thoughts and feelings into your partner's hands. So it is wise to see how kindly and carefully they, and you, are handled before going on to disclose more.

You should also add a reassuring note and say that just because you're talking about a fantasy doesn't mean that the two of you (or, indeed, the three or more of you) have to do it. (Incidentally, if you don't have fantasies, don't worry. Many people don't have them.)

Sexual fantasies come in all shapes and sizes. Children play "doctor," while their parents fantasize about group sex, making love on the beach, rock stars, visiting potentates, harem queens, empresses with slaves, streetwalkers, swapping partners, three in a bed, rapists and rape victims, seducing famous actors, schoolteachers punishing unruly students, Attila the Hun with the captured village beauty, door-to-door salesmen visiting passionate housewives.

Fantasies can be the portals of discovery and the basis for really beautiful intimacy. It's almost as if a fantasy shared is the ultimate intimacy, a secret world where only you and your lover enter, as naked of defenses as Adam and Eve, in a garden of discovery.

I'd like to show you one couple acting out their fantasy. Fantasies are so personal and individual you might dislike this one. That's fine. I'm certainly not recommending that you try this or any other specific fantasy. But I think it is useful to know how detailed a fantasy can be, what extraordinary risks two people can take when they are accepting and willing to be vulnerable, and what intense passion they find in their adventure.

If you decide to share a fantasy, the first step is to gather as much detail as possible. This may take time, and your partner may be embarrassed at first.

But the details do count. Be specific. Are there tassels on the boots? Is there music? Are there candles, bright lights? And then what happens? And then?

Acting out a fantasy is too involved for everyday love-making. It should be a kind of special occasion you save for birthdays, a sensual holiday, the longest night of winter, or an especially boring Tuesday.

You will need as much privacy as possible. You might consider a place away from home, where the phone won't ring. Or take the phone off the hook.

Start simply, doing things gradually, adding more as you gain confidence and it becomes more enjoyable. Above all, don't do anything that makes you uncomfortable.

One common male fantasy (and increasingly common for women) is bondage — being dominated, tied up, and treated like a slave by a partner whose sole concern is self-pleasure. The reason why bondage is attractive to some men seems clear: it can be a great relief for a man not to have to be responsible for initiating and orchestrating lovemaking. Especially when he knows that his partner's primary concern is self-pleasure. Besides, the teasing of bondage adds to the intensity of his sensations. And the visual effects and verbal taunts can be outrageously erotic.

Cathy and Pete have been lovers for two years. Cathy is a vivacious sales representative for a metropolitan TV station. Pete runs his own construction company.

They are in Pete's house in a suburb of Seattle. The lights are low, and candles give the room a shadowy, flickering effect. They are just finishing a pipe of marijuana. (They find that marijuana enlarges their fantasies, and helps them laugh and play. Others, I hasten to add, find that marijuana enlarges their anxieties and inhibitions.)

They have decided that for tonight Cathy is the Queen of the Northwest, a woman whose realm extends over all of the United States except New York City, Washington, D.C., and

Miami. All that power has corrupted her somewhat and she is used to having her slightest wish instantly obeyed. Cathy leans over and whispers in Pete's ear: "From this moment on, I am in charge. You will do absolutely nothing without my permission." Pete chuckles. "No laughing. Not unless I tell you to," Cathy adds.

"Now, draw my bath." Cathy is firm, domineering, and demanding. "The water is too hot." "Now it's too cold." "Take my blouse off. But don't touch my body." As she slips into the tub, she instructs Pete to undress for her pleasure so she can watch him as she luxuriates in the warm, soapy water. She gives him detailed instructions about how to stroke himself as he undresses. When he is naked, she bids him approach the bath. Outside it's drizzling and sleeting. Neighbors are doing dishes and watching television. Here a great queen is being attended by her slave. "Soap my back. Good. Now my neck. Not my ears. I didn't tell you to do my ears. You do exactly what I tell you. That should be simple enough." As you see, the situation lends itself to some humiliation. Within the rules of the game and the context of fantasy, some like humiliation and some do not. Pete, it seems, likes just a little. "Soap my breast. Gently. Not *breasts,* breast."

When she emerges from her bath, clean and slippery, Pete, following her instructions, towels her dry. She is patted and rubbed as regally and as carefully as any monarch in history. "Go into my bedchamber and wait," she tells him.

Men, it seems, tend to be more visually sexually aroused than women. And women tend to be especially sensitive to the sensual feel of things. Of course there are exceptions, but Cathy now, as she dresses, is enjoying the sensual feel of silk and lace. And she is dressing for visual effect, for Pete. Cathy puts on black lacy stockings and a black garter belt. She puts on a lacy black bra. Over her garter belt she puts on pure silk black panties with lace trim. She puts on spike heels and a full-length slinky robe.

She gathers up some long silk scarves that she has laid out and strides into the bedroom. Though she is not a tall woman, Cathy's presence, in high heels, black, silk, and lace is startling. Pete is aroused by the sight of her. He is relaxing on the bed. "What are you doing on my bed? Get down on your knees."

Pete kneels in front of her and she comes very close to him. He can smell her perfume. He reaches out to touch the bareness of her inner thigh above her stocking: "Don't touch me. You will do nothing until I *tell* you to. Besides, I feel like touching myself."

Being in charge, taking the initiative and dominating, is more than a refreshing change for Cathy — it is exciting. At first, when they had started playing this fantasy, she felt quite shy and a little foolish. But as she began to exercise her will, gaining confidence and skill, she began to be aware of how much pleasure was available to her just for the asking. She found that some of the things that she never would have imagined herself doing, far from making her anxious, as she had feared, were actually arousing to her. She also felt an added dimension of pleasure from her lover's rising, helpless excitement.

Striding up and down in front of Pete, in and out of shadows, sometimes stopping to extend a leg and pose, sometimes cupping a breast, sometimes running her hands slowly all over her body, sometimes touching herself through her panties, Cathy begins to strip. She takes off her bra and panties, constantly teasing Pete, saying "Wouldn't you like to touch me here?" "I'll bet your tongue would like to be doing what my finger is doing." Her robe open, in heels, stockings, and garter belt, she stands inches away from him. "I want a lot of pleasure tonight. I expect a great deal of pleasure from you. Caress my thigh . . . Give me a lot of pleasure . . . That's enough."

"Now touch yourself. Hold your penis in your hand. Stroke yourself. Faster. Now slowly. Show me how you like to touch yourself. Yes, like that . . . you seem to be very excited. Stop."

One of the great elements of doing this fantasy is teasing. Doing a little, then stopping. Verbally baiting your partner ("I'll bet you'd like to be inside me now, wouldn't you? Well, I'm not ready yet. I want a lot more pleasure first").

Something about the way Pete touches Cathy's stomach "displeases" her. As "punishment," she ties his hands and feet to the bed with silk scarves. She kneels over him and commands him to give her pleasure by kissing her breasts and her clitoris. Her instructions are detailed and specific. As soon as he becomes aroused she tells him to stop. She is merciless in her teasing. Several times, touching him, stimulating him with her hands, mouth, breasts, or hair, she brings him very close to orgasm. (But, as she tells him, he's not allowed to have an orgasm yet.) Always, she stops him just short of orgasm, so that his mounting excitement is almost unbearable. She mixes pleasure and pain, pinching his nipples and squeezing his testicles. (It's important to note that you should have a safety-valve signal that means "stop," since it's not always possible to distinguish between your partner's pleasure and pain.) Cathy is in complete command, occasionally untying a hand as a "reward." "Touch me here . . . I want more pleasure . . . That's enough. Kiss me here. Use your tongue . . . Stop."

Pete's rising pleasure excites her. She unties him, commands him to stand up, and ties his hands behind his back. He watches her closely as she masturbates herself to orgasm and listens to her describe how good it would feel to have his penis thrusting inside her. She gives him very specific instructions for her own pleasure, about how to touch and kiss and lick. She acts like a queen — *her* needs come first. She has several orgasms while reminding Pete that he must wait for his — if indeed she's going to allow him to have one at all.

When, at last, with Pete's hands and feet tied up, she takes his penis inside her, his whole body has been incredibly sexually sensitized. And so has hers. She withdraws from him.

"Not so fast. I want you to go very slowly." Later, she gives him permission to have an orgasm. Just before he ejaculates, she unties his legs as a practical precaution against his straining his leg muscles or tearing the scarves.

If you had listened very closely, you might have heard both Pete and Cathy tell each other, from time to time, that they love each other. For them, acting out a fantasy is a means of giving each other the most intimate pleasure possible — a gift of love.

The wild, even savage orgasm they both have leaves them with a feeling of peace. They feel very close to each other now. They've left their fantasy roles and are holding each other in the calm after a storm, kissing each other quietly and saying words we cannot hear.

Later, they will talk about what they will add, leave out, or change in the fantasy the next time.

Fantasies have been with us long enough to be recognized as part of the human condition. Down through the millennia they have been both suppressed and celebrated. Whether or not someone in ancient history or in downtown Boston has had sexual fantasies similar to yours is really beside the point. Fantasies are highly individual, often unique. That's what makes them so private and so special. And that's why sharing your sexual fantasy with someone you love can be a very tender intimacy.

Intimacy is so rare and so worthwhile. It is, in a sense, the ultimate luxury, a special place in an often hostile world, where you can gain emotional strength and make love grow. Intimacy is exposing all sides of yourself, even the side that wants, for example, to be tied up in silk scarves. It's a risky position, for you have given away all your defenses. If I had to put a single definition on sexual confidence, I suppose I might say that it is the courage to be accepting and vulnerable. Those three qualities — courage, being accepting, and being vulnerable — give you passage into intimacy.

14

Footnotes for the Future

Where did pleasure get its dirty name?

Pleasure is the opposite of pain. Pleasure inhibits anxiety. Pleasure reduces guilt. Sexual pleasure, according to one cardiologist, helps prevent heart disease. Perhaps if pleasure didn't feel so good, we might feel better about it.

Perhaps if pleasure hurt, we'd call it a virtue.

Three and a half centuries after Plymouth Rock, Puritan morality lingers on. We no longer put our neighbors in stockades or drown "witches." But we are still wary of pleasure. The Puritans thought pleasure was the devil's work. The nineteenth-century historian Lord Macaulay noted that "The Puritan hated bear-baiting, not because it gave pain to the bear, but because it gave pleasure to the spectators."

We no longer believe that pleasure is worse than animal torture. But despite sexual freedom and the "age of self," many people still feel uneasy about the idea of heightened sexual pleasure. And to tell one's children that sexual pleasure is wonderful — that's going too far, isn't it?

What you tell your children is a reflection of your own beliefs. So it is important, I think, first to define what you feel about pleasure.

Children grow up, summer runs into fall, our old pleasures

drain away, and at some moment, years or moments from now, you will yield all your pleasures to death. Dr. Samuel Johnson, the great eighteenth-century writer, said, "Life admits not of delays; when pleasure can be had, it's fit to catch it. Every hour takes away part of the things that please us, and perhaps part of our disposition to be pleased." Ill, poor, and alone for most of his life, Dr. Johnson's pleasures were few. Perhaps that is what gave him his insight. That time will steal all our pleasures from us makes our pleasures all the more precious.

Most people, said one philosopher, lead "lives of quiet desperation." Their jobs are unrewarding, there is rarely enough money, the future is uncertain, and the past is gone. Against so grim a backdrop as the evening news, sexual pleasure might almost seem a moral duty, an affirmation of life, joy in a world that broadcasts disaster.

Of course there is more to pleasure than seizing the moment, as Dr. Johnson suggests. Seizing the moment may hurt someone, or exploit someone, or be hopelessly irresponsible. And pleasurable moments aren't always there for the seizing. Sometimes they have to be created and lovingly nurtured.

Sexual confidence is the ability to create and enjoy sexual pleasure. Sexual confidence is going slowly. Gradually. Step by step. Talking. Learning. Laughing. Letting pleasure displace anxiety and pain. Being accepting. Being vulnerable. Being intimate.

Sexual pleasure weaves its way into every step of sexual confidence. Pleasure is the incentive and the reward. Pleasure is the antidote for anxieties and pain. Pleasure scatters demons to the winds.

Pleasure is what you create and give — a gift that returns to you to share.

But even if you accept the virtue and value of pleasure, one question still remains. What do you tell the children?

SEXUAL CONFIDENCE IN FRONT OF
THE CHILDREN

We've already seen that most sex education, in emphasizing procreation and disease, leaves out most of sexuality: pleasure, love and affection, caresses and playfulness, talking and laughing. In leaving out intimacy and pleasure and focusing on mechanics, most sex education encourages impersonal, mechanical sex, or "just screwing," as one unhappy young woman put it.

As a parent, I'm very conscious of the parental predicament: most parents don't mean to be secretive about sex, but they are uncomfortable with the subject. And they may fear that being open and telling the whole story of pleasure and desire will lead their children into promiscuity and emotional harm — as if sexual knowledge leads to moral weakness.

In fact, if a child is led to believe that his/her parents are not sexual, the child is apt to think sex is furtive and dirty. That sex is something that "nice" people like his parents don't engage in. If a child doesn't have access to realistic and correct sexual knowledge at home, the child is apt to assume that the sexual myths of the street corner and the schoolyard are fact. Those myths, rather than preventing promiscuity, lead a child into sex without pleasure and add to the risk of adolescent pregnancy.

The answer to the parent's predicament, I think, lies in accepting the fact that somewhere, sometime your child will be involved in sex. It may be sooner than you wish, it may be later than you might wish. But now, when your children are young, may be the only time you can exercise your parental protectiveness of your child's sexuality. By protectiveness I don't mean shielding them, but giving them the strength to develop their own protection. Now you can give your children the knowledge and confidence to cope with peer pressure, trends, and fads. Now you can give them a sense of the beauty and the pleasure of their sexuality. Giving your children sound sexual knowledge at a very early age not only will stand them in good stead now, but also can be part of the basis for a wise, accepting, and loving life in the future, free from the impediments of myth, anxiety, and guilt.

I've painted a somewhat idealized goal here. You may not be able to give your children all that you would like. For children have minds of their own. Some children listen to their parents and some don't. Some are carefree, some thoughtful, some cautious, some are influenced by friends, and some won't listen to anybody. All are complex individuals with worlds of their own. Of course they scrape their knees and bloody their noses. Children and adolescents try things you wish they wouldn't and make wrong choices. And, after all, a parent is human, too. There are bound to be mistakes on both sides. No one is perfect, thank heavens. But here, for better or for worse, is my own outline for giving your children sexual confidence. My usual proviso is attached: These are suggestions, not rules. If something here makes you uncomfortable, don't do it. Or if it seems difficult, but you think it might be worth trying, try doing just a little bit of it, slowly, gradually, one step at a time.

Infants and Children

Sexuality begins soon after birth. Along with fingers and toes a baby discovers genitals. You can actually encourage your children's self-exploration. Leave the diapers off from time to time. Give babies play time in the bathtub, where they can discover how good it feels to touch not only their genitals but their whole body.

Later, when they are older, they may touch their genitals and say how good it feels, or just "mmmmm." Encourage that. Or at least don't discourage it. Taking pleasure in your own body is the first essential step toward feeling good about yourself. Besides, it is fun. To be sure, you should also teach your child that the time and place for masturbation is not everywhere. As the British educator A. S. Neill said to his daughter, the place for masturbation is your own bedroom — or your own garden.

As a way of showing your children that the body is something to be comfortable with instead of something always to cover up and hide, you might quite naturally be nude or only partially dressed in front of them from time to time. Do this only if you feel relaxed and comfortable about it, or everybody will feel uneasy.

If your child walks in while you are nude or dressing, act as natural as you can. Don't treat it as a special occasion. Similarly, if a child wanders in while you are making love, you can be perfectly straightforward: "Hello, darling. We're making love now and we like to do this in private. Please go out and shut the door."

You might also be direct when you are talking about parts of the body. When a child asks "What's that?," use the correct words: "That's my penis." "That's your vagina." "Those are my breasts." Cute or evasive nicknames like "pee pee" or "down there" tend to communicate that these are things to be squeamish about, unlike a toe or a nose.

If you read to your child at bedtime, it's a good idea to intersperse books about sexuality along with *Winnie-the-Pooh*. *How Babies Are Made,* by A. C. Andry and S. Schepp (Time-Life Books, 1968), may seem a strange bedtime fellow for *Winnie-the-Pooh*. But reading is a nice, easy, informative way to bring up the topic of sex, free from the possible embarrassment and drama that a child's first sexual question sometimes causes ("Mommy, what does 'fuck' mean?").

As resident hero, and more or less live-in god, it is important for you to let your child know that you are sexual. You and your spouse can kiss passionately in front of the children. Let them know that you enjoy it. When you're reading about the making of babies, you can tell them that making love is something that *you* do, adding that you do it in private. Mention the pleasure, and talk about affection and love. Say that people make love because it's wonderful and fun and because they love each other. And also, by the way, that's the way they make babies.

The details of what you talk about — what, precisely, you say about sex — don't matter nearly so much as establishing sex as an everyday topic. If sex is as open a topic as the news, sports, and weather, then questions and problems related to sex can be discussed at the dinner table.

When children go off to school they are exposed to new values. Even if you have taught them about the pleasure of their bodies, the beauty of sexuality, the equality of the sexes — all of those carefully nurtured values may be swept aside by the onrush of the rest of the world into the classroom. Boys discover shame and try to look under girls' skirts. Girls cover up their bodies and wonder what boys look like under their trousers. In many ways your children will conform to the values of their peers or the locker room. What is important, I think, is that you remain consistent in talking about sex openly. Even if your children appear not to care about what you say, your openness will be remembered and called upon later. When children feel their own bodies changing, hear the usual sexual rumors, and feel that they are abnormal or weird, if there's an open forum on sex at home, they'll be more likely to come to you for reliable information.

Adolescents

In discussions about sex you can begin to tell a child prior to and during adolescence about the complexities of life: that some people live together and are not married, that some people have affairs, that some people are heterosexual, that some people are homosexual, that some people are bisexual. You are not advocating a point of view but rather educating your child about how complicated sex and love and relationships can be.

If you've had sex before marriage you might say so, and talk about the way you made that decision. If you waited until marriage for sex, you might talk about that decision. Even if your children don't make decisions the way you do (and they probably won't), you can give them a sense of your value system. There's a fine line here between your own privacy and saying too much. There is, after all only so much a child wants to hear, and only so much you want to say. One way to keep your privacy and avoid embarrassment is to talk openly but not about yourself. You might comment about a movie, about what other people do, what it was like when you grew up, and how times have or have not changed.

In the same vein, if there is a divorce or a separation don't try to shield your children, let them know why it happened. You don't have to give all the details, but you should communicate a sense of the complexity. You are giving the children useful maps to use in their own lives. Without those maps you leave your children without reference points in a world that is indeed highly complex.

Some children may feel intimidated by a world that isn't simple. And some rebel against their parents' being so open by becoming more sexually conservative than their parents. Also, it's often difficult for people to talk about their intimate feelings. Many of the feelings of the young are brand new to them, they are embarrassed (as you may be), they lack the words, and they may reject your efforts to talk. There's no need to push them. Empathize with their awkwardness. And try to remember that they are not rejecting you so much as they are trying to find their own identities.

I am an advocate of the forum of the dinner table (or the kitchen or living room or bedside or car). Topics such as masturbation and wet dreams, which should be discussed as early as possible, can be very difficult to bring up. You could sit the child down and begin a kind of lecture, but that's apt to be embarrassing to both of you. The dinner table, on the other hand, lends itself to casual conversation. You might, for example, mention that historically, before the Kinsey report in 1948, people suspected that they were sick or abnormal when they masturbated or had wet dreams or homosexual thoughts. Then Kinsey showed that many things that people had thought were strange, unhealthy behavior — including masturbation, wet dreams, homosexuality, and sexual fantasies of all kinds — were really quite normal. They are all a very common part of human experience.

The subject of sex comes up from all directions, from school, TV, movies, and your own children ("Hey, I just found out my homeroom teacher is gay"). Talking about sex as part of the news from school, world affairs, or office politics can reduce a lot of the tension surrounding the subject.

At the dinner table parents can also bring up a subject and talk about it to each other, subjects such as lovemaking or marriage or teen-age sex. The children don't have to join in the conversation. Many times they won't. But they usually listen to every word.

If there is to be even a remote chance that your children will assimilate your values, they need to know what your values are and how you feel about them. And they will also need to have some guidelines in how to express their own feelings about sex. Knowing what their parents think and feel about sex can be a very important guide to children both for developing their own value systems and for expressing their sexual feelings.

The subject of contraception should come up for discussion quite early, certainly before high school.

This is a difficult subject for many parents. In fact, some parents feel that discussing contraception openly is tantamount to giving approval to their children's having intercourse.

While recognizing that contraception is controversial, I think that it is also important to acknowledge that adolescents will probably be sexually active with or without your approval. Whether or not they have intercourse, and where, and when, and with whom are all decisions you would like to make for them. But they are all decisions you cannot make. What you can do, however, is make sure that at an early age your child is equipped with knowledge about contraception. For if you can't prevent adolescent sex, you can help to prevent adolescent pregnancies.

Along with advice and guidance about the physiology of sex, you can also tell adolescents about vulnerability, sharing, acceptance, and communication. You can help them define their own ideas of a good relationship, and give them some sense of the emotions and responsibilities that are a part of sex.

Adolescence is a very difficult time for children. It may be even harder on their parents. Adolescence is almost always turbulent, almost always a time of revolution. Inevitably kids discard, temporarily or even permanently, what their parents hold most dear: their value system. It's very hard for a parent to accept this. You can make your feelings known in no uncertain terms; you can set rules; but in many ways the adolescent is on his or her own. And the best way you have of keeping the lines of communication open is to be accepting. That may be very difficult. Accepting hair that's too long or too short, accepting that your "baby" is involved with someone you disapprove of or is having sex before he or she (or you) is emotionally ready, or chooses a sexual preference you find sinful, can be almost impossibly difficult. But acceptance is part of intimacy and love.

If you have a son, there's one chance in ten that he will be gay. And at least one out of every three males experiments with homosexual sex. The odds are not quite so high for your daughter's being homosexual, but the possibility is just as real.

No one knows why some people are homosexual and some are not. It may simply be part of the natural order of things. In any case, your child will need your support rather than your rejection. And if your child is gay and you cannot give acceptance and love — whether or not you approve of his or her sexual preference — you may lose your child.

Lately I've been finding that more teen-agers and young adults, perhaps one-third, are choosing not to have intercourse before marriage. Everybody isn't "doing it." (It's too soon to tell if this is a significant trend.) It's interesting that they have to resist the tide of their friends' pressure. What a difference from the school days of their parents, when most teen-agers were expected to be virgins. Now young men and women who choose to remain "chaste" until marriage or love may need to wage a lonely and repetitious battle. If there is an open forum at home, if they can talk about sex with their parents, they can get the support that they need.

Why is it sometimes so difficult to talk to our teen-aged offspring? Well, they are often difficult, moody, remote, and irrational in turns. But also we tend to become a little stodgy and inflexible when we become parents. Perhaps it's just a natural result of the enormous responsibility for another life and of the enormous love we feel. Whatever it is, something makes it very difficult for us to remember our own feelings of frustration and isolation when we were rebelling against our own parents. Reviving those feelings, remembering the risks you took and the mistakes you had to make, can go some way toward bridging the gap between you and your child. But even so, the gap, tragic though it may seem, will still be there to some degree. And acceptance is the only bridge you may have, the only alternative to alienation when everything you say and try is rejected.

But in a larger sense the bridge you have is sexual confidence. Having opened the doors of understanding on the most difficult subjects at the most trying times, you're apt to be close to your child in a deep and fundamental way. And having taken risks and ventured into the emotional and sexual unknown yourself, you can help your child to laugh at the slips and mishaps that are a part of your child's emotional journey. In a sense, the bridge between you and your children is a bridge of the imagination, but a bridge you will, by this time, be able to cross.

Having learned to unlearn sexual myths, anxiety, and guilt, and having learned to value your own strengths and the importance of intimacy and romance, it can be an enormous pleasure to lead your own child out of the old repressive circle between Victorian shame and impersonal, performance-oriented sex — to help your child join the new sexual revolution called sexual confidence.

For sexual confidence is sharing dreams and sharing laughter, with your partner and with your children.

Sexual confidence is sharing the pleasure of life.

INDEX

Index